Published by TechnologyPress, Orlando, FL.

Printed in the United States of America.

ISBN: 978-0-9980369-2-2
LCCN: 2019936919

This publication is designed to provide accurate and authoritative information with regard to the subject matter covered. It is sold with the understanding that the publisher is not engaged in rendering legal, accounting, or other professional advice. If legal advice or other expert assistance is required, the services of a competent professional should be sought. The opinions expressed by the authors in this book are not endorsed by TechnologyPress and are the sole responsibility of the author rendering the opinion.

Most TechnologyPress titles are available at special quantity discounts for bulk purchases for sales promotions, premiums, fundraising, and educational use. Special versions or book excerpts can also be created to fit specific needs.

For more information, please write:
TechnologyPress
520 N. Orlando Ave, #2
Winter Park, FL 32789
or call 1.877.261.4930

TechnologyPress
Winter Park, Florida

CONTENTS

CHAPTER 1

WHY SMALL BUSINESSES ARE A CYBERCRIMINAL'S #1 TARGET

BY RUSSELL POUCHER

The dependency of our society and economy to rely on IT is increasing daily. Cybersecurity affects organizations ranging from small and medium-sized businesses to educational institutions and government agencies. Across the board, business owners, managers, and directors are seeking stronger cybersecurity and safer ways of protecting their organizations.

According to StaySafeOnline.org, attacks on small businesses now account for over 70% of all data breaches. This is a number that only continues to rise. Close to half of all small businesses have been compromised, and ransomware attacks alone have skyrocketed an alarming 250% since 2016. Additionally, as reported by *Media Planet*, increased incidents of phishing have also followed suit.

Cybersecurity has become such a threat, that as of 2019, Managed Services Providers, better known as "MSP's," have now been issued regulations by the Department of Homeland Security.

DON'T BELIEVE THE MYTH OF:
"IT WON'T HAPPEN TO ME."

Small and medium-sized businesses often think that they won't become the target of a cyber threat. But this is a very dangerous lie to believe, and leaves businesses at risk. Generally speaking, cybercriminals are actually targeting small businesses even more now – as these hackers know that too many businesses are left unprotected.

Small businesses are typically lax on security. Often their firewalls are weak, maybe only consumer grade – that is, if they even have one in place. Other common security errors include not updating passwords regularly, or worse yet, using weak passwords altogether.

Business owners also tend to lack the dedicated staff necessary to defend against attacks. And for many, cybersecurity just is not a high enough priority for them when compared to all the daily 'fires' being addressed. This costly mistake compounds the negative effects of poor cyber training.

PROFESSIONAL SERVICES TO MANAGED SERVICES

These are just a few of the reasons why I love what I do. My team and I get to help small businesses protect themselves from cybercrime. We just celebrated our twenty-third anniversary. I became involved in security about ten years ago, and began managing macOS cybersecurity approximately five years ago. Now, we are members of Infoguard, which is the FBI's cybersecurity division. We receive a lot of declassified material from the FBI and are fully aware of the kind of businesses being targeted. Being equipped with insight as to the kind of tools hackers are using to breach networks, this gives us first and upper-hand knowledge of how to prevent attacks.

When I started this company, we were focused primarily on the professional services; I later added training to the lineup of offerings. We soon incorporated our managed services in security, and it has been a huge addition to our offered services. This was a direct result of seeing that so many of our clients were unprepared for the cyber risks associated with small businesses.

Even some of our own clients who were not following our advice were experiencing getting breached. And so I thought, "Well, it's our job to really crack down and make sure that they follow our advice. So we better be the ones to do it for them." This way our clients could see the benefit of managed services before it was too late.

Originally we started out servicing creative businesses, including people that were doing photography, graphic design, printing and the like. We quickly recognized a common denominator among these professions – Apple computers. It was a shift that led us to adapt our business to become specialized and certified in treating Apple devices and technology.

And since Apple had really diversified and had become a brand name company among a variety of different industries, we saw that manufacturing was another sector that was really picking up on the Apple side of things; hence, the relationship began servicing manufacturers, too. Today, we are partnering with elective healthcare.

CYBER SECURITY FOR ELECTIVE HEALTHCARE

HIPAA governs all healthcare procedures, including electives. Such procedures are processed for cash payment outside of normal insurance coverage. This would include plastic surgery and some dental communities. We have found that many of our clientele in the elective healthcare sector, are preferred Mac users.

The threat of an attack in a medical environment is treated

seriously, so our tech support team is always ready to respond when our clients need us. We guarantee our clients a wait time of sixty seconds or less to connecting live with an engineer. With the confidence and ability to solve complex issues that most other IT firms cannot, many of our new clients will often call us in to remedy some of their very advanced threats.

As a result of the Apple training program that came in place for us, we received many referrals directly from Apple because of our certifications and relationship with them. While other IT firms were saying that a problem could not be fixed, we would come in to service the small business or practice and tell them, "Yes, we can fix that and here's how."

THE BENEFITS OF APPLE'S CERTIFICATION

When Apple first started doing their training for IT service providers, there were only nine of us that started in the pilot program. And the most IT firms that Apple ever trained was only eighteen different companies. So overall, there are less than a hundred certified Apple trainers in the United States.

We also have certifications that are comparable to the Microsoft Certified System Engineer, which is called Apple Certified System Administrator. And there were less than 200 people in the entire country that were able to achieve that certification. So that's a major distinction that I am proud to hold. I was called upon to contribute to the development of the curriculum for Apple, and it was taught in the United States, Europe, and Asia. So I can bring my vast experience and unique certifications with Apple to the benefits of my clients.

Apple devices and technology can be very complicated for IT firms that are not familiar with working on Apple machines. I've always considered Apple to be a very cloak-and-dagger company because they don't talk about a lot of their security features. In fact, as a trainer, I had to sign off on my contract with them that said I was never allowed to talk about the flaws in their operating system with my students, or mention competing products. Years later, they took that part out of their contract, because it was considered just too much of a competitive disadvantage.

So the knowledge that we get from our Apple training, and working with their engineers directly, has allowed us to fix most of these problems that most other IT firms have told small businesses that they couldn't fix.

WHAT SMALL BUSINESS OWNERS NEED TO DO

There are a number of easy ways you can begin protecting your small business today. For instance, you can start with a risk audit. Assess all of your infrastructure, and come up with recommendations to strengthen security. Then, issue a security-screening questionnaire to your vendors and secure and encrypt your Wi-Fi networks.

Here are some other tips to help you protect your small business:

- Encrypt data on all devices including servers, workstations, laptops, and mobile devices.

- Provide firewall security for Internet connections, with a fully licensed security suite.

- Clean machines regularly with the latest threat management software, including all web browsers, and operating systems.

- Update systems, then run maintenance and threat scans afterwards.

- Install security apps on all company mobile phones.

- Limit employee access to information with their unique user accounts, and ensure they use strong passwords.

- Add Multi-Factor Authentication to all of your services, including email.

- Don't ignore the physical security of your data, such as hard drives, thumb drives, computers and mobile devices.

- Back up your data, with one local copy and one additional copy in the cloud at a minimum.

- Check your backups and make sure there is no corrupted data. Also, check to make sure you know how to recover files.

- Be careful with email attachments to avoid ransomware or phishing attacks.

- Use a VPN to secure your connections remotely.

- Get cyber insurance for your small business.

Remember, most cyber-attacks happen due to employee error. A proactive commitment to consistently fulfilling these suggestions will strengthen your cybersecurity.

I'm very proud to say that all clients who have followed our advice have not been compromised. We are frequently called in to conduct forensics for law enforcement. And what we find on a regular basis is that some of those best practices I just mentioned for securing your technology are sorely missed or overlooked. Sadly, most small business owners don't know how to protect themselves with technology or they don't want the headache of trying to implement these suggestions.

Surprisingly, they just leave themselves vulnerable and unprotected. However, when that happens, these small businesses are left completely open to cyber-attack – the consequences of which could be devastating. In addition to regulatory fines, and customer blowback, the financial cost of solving the security issue can be too much of a financial burden for small businesses to bear. It may even put them completely out of business.

In fact, we just recently had a detective in our office because one of our clients who brought us in had discovered that their accounts had been compromised. Our involvement in the forensic activity was minimal, however, we discovered that the compromise was a direct result of employee mishandling of the company password list and improper use of such passwords.

That's one of the main reasons why we never recommend writing passwords down on sticky notes and leaving them on the desk or under a keyboard. We find passwords left in the open all the time – on monitors and keyboards and in the top desk drawer. Instead, it is highly recommended that all passwords be secured with some type of encrypted algorithm.

ABIDING THE CALIFORNIA PRIVACY LAW

Here in California, we have what is known as the California Privacy Law, and this is a significant thing for small businesses. When businesses are in breach of the California Privacy Law, it can carry some pretty hefty fines that can put a company out of business. Even HIPAA and PCI violations, and neglect to comply with other legal regulations, when breached, can come with penalties of $100,000 minimum fee per occurrence. Moreover, if you think about an attack like that on your small business, it can become very pricey and put a company totally out of business.

Right now HIPAA doesn't even have enough agents to go out and assess all their fines. However, I can tell you from personal experience, that if I spent four weeks and just traveled around to all the doctor's offices here in Orange County, where I live, I would probably find a security breach in every single office.

Now fortunately, when you are audited, you are given the

opportunity to declare how you are going to fix the vulnerabilities. But if you have been a victim of an egregious breach, fines are imposed. I have already seen two doctors' offices go out of business because they couldn't handle the fines.

Don't let this happen to you. Take action to protect your small business today. Don't believe the myth: "It'll never happen to me." Take precaution by following the steps I've outlined, and commit to protecting your small business from cybercrime.

About Russell

Russell Poucher, President and Founder of Creative Resources Technology Group, takes pride in the knowledge that his firm is committed to providing top-tier technical support, customer service and product knowledge to his customers. Russell Poucher helps his clients navigate the challenging world of Information Technology (IT) and cybersecurity. This allows them to focus on their organization's core competencies, keeping their entire infrastructure operational and fully efficient. Russell's passion for security and IT resulted in launching Creative Resources Technology Group (CRTG). Since 1996, CRTG has evolved into the premier Apple managed services, professional services and cybersecurity company in Southern California.

Prior to starting CRTG, Russell worked as a System Administrator for several leading pre-press firms in Orange and Los Angeles Counties. He has numerous certifications in networking, security and system administration with a specialty in the Apple platform. By combining his knowledge of the medical, pre-press and printing industries, Russell is able to provide fully integrated technical solutions to his customers. Since opening its doors in 1996, CRTG has been heralded for its unique blend of technical expertise and customer service.

CRTG is a trusted advisor to businesses, providing Apple platform-based solutions, technical expertise, and resources to help its clients achieve their goals and solve their IT problems that other service providers cannot. The guiding principles and core values that Russell holds closest to his heart are also upheld by the company:

- Open and honest communication
- Taking extreme ownership
- Working in an efficient and focused manner
- Gratitude for the opportunities that have been provided

Russell, a national speaker, has shared the stage with some of the top speakers in cybersecurity (Kevin Mitnick) and Information Technology (IT) ranks (Steve Jobs, Richard Branson) at some of the premier Apple events (MacTech, MacWorld).

As a writer and content developer, he has written books and training curriculum on topics from macOS to Windows, security, infrastructure, and Wi-Fi networking. He has been recruited by Apple (curriculum development, training, and speaking), Adobe (curriculum development and speaking) and Dell (securing down their macOS environment, internationally) over the last 18 years to help with several initiatives and projects, including:

1. Writing a curriculum for Apple's technical certification classes.
2. Being an Apple Certified Trainer.
3. Contracted as an Apple Professional Services Provider.
4. Overseeing the training of Apple Consultants from Orange to San Diego counties.

Connect with Russell at:
- russell@creativeresources.net
- https://www.linkedin.com/in/russellpoucher/

CHAPTER 2

THE HISTORY OF CYBERSECURITY, AND HOW IT IMPACTS THE FUTURE OF YOUR NETWORK SAFETY

BY GARY MONCK

In the old days of the Wild, Wild West, when Wells Fargo wanted to send a shipment of gold to California, they used stagecoaches to transport the cargo across the county. Well, the first trips made it ok. But in a short time, the bad guys figured out that the Wells Fargo stagecoach had a box of gold on it. So, they robbed it. After being a victim of multiple horse-drawn carriage hold-ups, Wells Fargo decided to put the gold shipment on a train. Well, as you may know, even though the first trips went ok, in time again, the bad guys realized that the gold was now on the train. And so, they robbed the train. This simple history lesson teaches us a lot about the importance of cybersecurity, network privacy, and protecting your valuable information.

Things evolve. Technology changes. But with enough time and persistence, the bad guys will always become privy to new safety measures, and will find ways to breach the security clearance. Even though every business is at threat, if you are a small business, you are really a target for cybercrime. In fact, I would go as far as to say that if you are a small business, you are even more of a target for cyberattack, than a large business. Research shows, that consistently, small businesses are at a higher percentage of vulnerability to cyber attack.

Today, we are near the end of the Wild, Wild West days of the Internet. Security, and the assumption of security, are often two very different things. Cybercrime, like all crime, is a constant threat to our society and businesses alike. If you store confidential information of any kind, keep digital financial records, or are a vendor to local, state or the federal government in any capacity, you may be a target. The reality is, if you have anything important at all saved on your network and server, you really do need to protect it. You have to employ stricter, more stringent and more effective security measures to get the job done in your business, and to protect your clients and suppliers sensitive information at the same time.

HISTORY'S LESSONS TO PROTECT YOUR FUTURE

Cybercrime has gone back to the days when people used the Abacus. And because many people consider the Abacus to be the first "computer", technically speaking then, you could say that cybercrime has been around for hundreds of years! And modern cybercrime started when people were doing "phone phreaking" in the late 1950s. Perhaps the most famous of "phone phreaks" was Kevin Mitnick, who from the mid-1970s until 1995, breached some incredibly secure networks, including Motorola and Nokia. So cybercrime has been around a lot longer than most people think.

In fact, the news media just recently reported on a cybercrime that had its thirty-year anniversary. In 1988, the "Morris Worm" accidentally got out of the Massachusetts Institute of Technology, and it's creator, Robert Morris, became the first person to get convicted for violating the Computer Fraud and Abuse Act.

As this brief history of cybercrime shows, the danger of attack is real. And while many of these crimes were initially committed by very intelligent teenagers who happened to use their powers to prank, in short order the severity of these crimes took a turn for the worse. The malicious intent of cybercriminals puts any website, network, or server at risk. Cyberattacks can cause a dismal effect on your business.

REGULATORS ARE CRACKING DOWN

In an attempt to thwart potential online criminals, the Federal government along with other national and international organizations, are cracking down on cybersecurity. Regulators ranging from the United States Congress, and the Payment Card Industry Data Security Standard, to the General Data Protection Regulation, or "GDPR" in Europe are enforcing stricter policies. Even health care and medical fields are tightening regulations on HIPAA requirements.

For instance, last year, the U.S. Federal Government put into effect regulations that said anybody that sells to the Fed has to comply with a basic set of standards of protecting their network information, via cybersecurity, so that a breach will not occur. The Department of Defense came up with a list of very stringent, expensive, and time-consuming regulations that vendors now have to comply with. And that is true whether suppliers sell them anything – from a physical widget to a piece of software. Basically, anybody involved in the supply chain has to comply with this new set of standards, and mind you, they are daunting.

Additionally, states such as New York, Massachusetts and Maryland have already passed laws, and other states are following suit, which dictate that if there is a breach of your company's network, you have to notify the state officials. My hypothesis is that in the next year or so, like the Federal Government, these states will also create a list of things that you have to do to be in business. More than likely, this will be a very specific set of standards that are enforced in order to protect your customer's and employee information alike.

This is the "present-future" of online business regulations. It is already the case if you sell to the government, and it is increasingly so if you sell to any city and state clients. Even in a business-to-business or business-to-consumer market, strengthening cybersecurity will continue to include a tightening down, with a stricter standard of business. Therefore, in order for you to beat the curve, and be ahead of the competition in terms of compliance with regulatory standards, you should be implementing a cybersecurity plan within your own business as well.

STEPS TO PREVENT CYBERCRIME

Luckily, the tools that are available to us now for cybersecurity are at a much more affordable cost than what they were even just a few years ago. We do have the tools to start fighting this. When I work with new clients, the first place we start in implementing a cybersecurity plan is with a risk assessment. We will go through their entire business, and look at things from technology and non-technology alike. We will find out where they are the most vulnerable, and we will come up with a plan of action. We will create specific milestones and work through that plan, filling in the largest holes we come across, in order to get the biggest bang for our buck.

The plan to improve your cybersecurity is never-ending. Here is a short checklist of items to begin considering:

- Security and Risk Assessment – Establish a security baseline and assess web address vulnerabilities

- Computer Updates – Keep your computer operating system and software up to date. Install patches and updates as needed.

- Back It Up – Follow the "321 Rule": Three backups, two media types and one offsite mode. Do not forget to test your backups often.

- Firewall – Use a business class firewall and subscribe to Intrusion Detection (IDS) and Intrusion Prevention (IPS) Services.

- Secure Email – Protect your email from spam, phishing, virus, malware, and identity theft.

- Passwords and Authentication – Implement strong password policies and multi-factor authentication on systems and applications.

- Ongoing Training – Continually educate your team members on proper security protocol, cyber awareness and be sure to test all users regularly.

MAKE CYBER-PROTECTION PART OF YOUR BUSINESS DNA

All through my life I've been interested in technology. I have been in this field for thirty years. So, I have been following the Internet and computers and security for a long time. And I am old enough to remember when computers were the newest thing. As a kid, I remember my parents sending me to the Maryland Academy of Science. There, I saw a computer that was as large as the room. I remember experimenting with it and learned how to start programming it to do basic calculations. That was my initial foray into technology and computer security. As I would play around and test things with that computer, I would learn more.

As I got older, my love for technology continued. While in college at the University of Maryland, Baltimore County, I studied biochemistry. On top of that, my father was a World War II vet. So, I guess you could say that the nature to defend and protect is in my DNA. In some way, I look at my work in cybersecurity, data protection, and online defense, as a way of continuing my father's legacy.

I have been teaching the importance of cybersecurity for years and have helped many people stay safe online. A lot of times, people and companies make the false assumption that just because a technology store or a large retailer sells them a computer, or some other Internet device, that it is safe. Or maybe they will think that just because a tech company would make an online product or software, that it was ok. But in modern days, we have learned that this is not always the case.

Take the step today to strengthen your online security. Seek out professional help, as you and your small business need it. Because protecting your sensitive information with a stricter cybersecurity plan is not just the wave of the future, it is the current reality we all live in now.

About Gary

Gary Monck is on a mission to help businesses keep cybersecurity and compliance simple, safe, secure, and successful. As CEO and founder of Cispoint, Inc., Gary brings the knowledge and expertise of enterprise-grade support and tools to small and mid-sized businesses. A technology expert with over thirty years of experience, Gary has the unique ability to translate highly technical processes and procedures into easy-to-understand terms for business owners, executives, and employees.

At an early age, Gary's parents sent him to a summer program at The Maryland Academy of Sciences for an introduction to programming. The program was the beginning of his interest in technology. As a son of a Disabled American Veteran, Gary was exposed to the advanced technology of the early years of kidney dialysis. The rapidly expanding and advancement in technology added fifteen years to his father's life. While attending the University of Maryland-Baltimore County, Gary worked in the emergency room as a technician, where he met his wife, Jennifer.

Gary holds multiple CompTIA, Microsoft, and vendor certifications. Technology, cybersecurity, and compliance are both his hobby and passion. Gary enjoys sharing his knowledge and experiences as a local and national speaker. As an instructor at a local college of technology, he taught Microsoft technologies to students entering their IT careers.

Gary is focused on making the complex technologies of cybersecurity, and compliance:

- **Simple** to implement
- Provide a **Safe** computing environment
- **Secure** your network resources

So your business can be **Successful**!

CHAPTER 3

THE MOST POPULAR WAYS CYBERCRIMINALS HACK YOUR NETWORK

BY CARL SCALZO

This book has shown several ways you can protect your business from the many threats to IT security. Now, with my chapter, I am going to recap some of the most popular ways that cybercriminals can hack your network and wreak havoc on your life. More importantly, I will quickly review action steps you can take to prevent these attacks.

BEST PRACTICES FOR PASSWORDS

You may think that your passwords are clever or complicated when they are filled with exclamation points and other random numbers. But the truth is that it's rarely enough. With information gathered from social engineering or social media accounts, hackers can easily use brute-force to figure out what your password is.

Brute-Force Password Attacks are when a hacker guesses your password. They can do this by either using software, that after inputting some basic data about the target, will run through potential keys ad infinitum. With sufficient information about the target, it's only a matter of time before the software figures out your password.

More often than that, hackers can simply guess the password. Infiltrators have common passwords that use real words or common structures memorized and can run through hundreds of sign-on attempts before giving up.

EMAIL

(1). Spam

Also known as junk email, spam is any unsolicited messages sent out in bulk email.

Many of these spam emails contain disguised links that appear to be for known websites, but are in fact a link to phishing sites or other sites hosting malware that can infect your network.

(2). Spoofing

Refers to hackers tricking you or your system. This type of deception is typically done when a hacker hides the sender's identity, or fakes the identity of another user, when sending messages. This may involve sending messages from a bogus email address or faking the email address of another user.

Hackers understand that you're much more likely to read a message from an address you know, so they'll often spoof addresses to trick you into taking an action that you would not normally take with an unknown address.

A good way to confirm emails would be to hover your mouse over the sender's email address to verify that it is indeed coming from someone you know.

The four most common actions that hackers will try to get you to take are:

i. Replying to the message - including sending an unsubscribed answer.

ii. Clicking any hyperlink in the message - that includes the unsubscribe link.

iii. Opening an attachment.

iv. Forwarding the email message on to others.

Hackers will try to make their requests sound urgent so that you take immediate action, especially to avoid a negative consequence or to mitigate a threat.

They will also try to entice you to click by offering something of value, which again, is part of their scam. Or they may ask you to resolve an urgent problem. So be sure to stay aware and not click on anything that's not legitimate.

Additionally, do NOT open email attachments that end with: .exe, .scr, .bat, .com or other executable files that you do not recognize. If you are uncertain, you should pick up the phone and call the sender to confirm.

(3). Phishing

This is fake email masquerading as legitimate. Hackers create phishing emails to steal confidential information. Generally, a phishing scheme appears to have come from a known person or organization, like your bank or your boss.

These emails try creating a sense of urgency. They want you to panic in order to trick you into giving them personal details. For example, if you receive an email from your bank saying that your ATM card has been disabled and you need to confirm your card number or enter your PIN into a website to reactivate it. A victim who has received this email might think that it is legitimate, when in reality this email has been sent from a hacker trying to steal your information.

Phishing emails may also contain a link to which clicking on it will take you to a fake web page. For example, the link might take you to a fake bank website which looks legitimate, but in reality, is just a malicious lookalike. If the victim falls for the scam and enters their account details on this false website, then their details will go to the hacker's server, instead of going to the bank. That way, the hacker will have all the information that the victim has provided on the website.

Another way hackers use phishing is that the email may have an attachment that asks you to download it. As soon as you click on it and begin downloading, it releases malware that installs on your device, giving the hacker complete access to your device and data.

Some tips for spotting phishing emails include looking for spelling and grammatical errors within domain names or email addresses of the message. Cybercriminals often use email addresses that resemble the names of well-known companies, but are slightly altered in order to be more believable.

For example: User@gmall.com instead of User@gmail.com.

Secondly, think twice before clicking any links. If you see a link in a suspicious email message, don't click on it. Instead, hover your mouse over it to see if the URL matches the link that was provided in the message.

Cybercriminals often use threats saying that your security has been compromised or your account has been blocked. Don't fall for such tricks. Take your time to assess the situation and to determine if a real compromise has indeed happened.

(4). Spear Phishing

This is a form of phishing where the attack specifically targets an individual or group. Since the attacker has researched the target and crafted their attack accordingly, spear phishing attacks are more likely to succeed. Spear phishing emails are often the source of APT's.

(5). Advanced Persistent Threats (APT's)

This refers to a prolonged, stealth attack that is generally difficult to detect and may go on for months before being discovered.

SOCIAL ENGINEERING

Hacking that uses real, well-intentioned people to carry out its schemes. This is especially effective for gathering sensitive information.

For example, say your IT company receives a call from the "employee" of one of your clients, pretending that they're experiencing problems that your IT professional is more than happy to help with. Well, before you know it, the caller knows all the ins-and-outs of your entire security system, or lack thereof.

Social engineers have also been known to use phone company customer service departments, Facebook and other services to gather Social Security or credit card numbers.

SMISHING

This is a form of phishing in which a hacker tries to trick you into giving them your private information via a phone call or SMS message. Smishing is becoming an emerging and growing threat in the world of online security.

Smishing uses elements of social engineering to get you to share your personal information. This tactic leverages your trust in order to obtain your information. The information an attacker is looking for can be anything from an online password to your bank account details or One Time Passwords to gain access to your accounts.

Once the hacker has your required data, he can use it for various attacks. Messages sometimes also come with shortened links with luring offers and deals, that when clicked, install malware on your devices.

The best way to prevent smishing is by not sharing any critical information over a phone call or in SMS.

Also, you want to always verify the identity of the message before clicking links in it. And if you receive a message saying it's from a person you know, and it asks you for critical data, call the person on the number stored in your contacts, instead of calling the SMS number, and verify that he/she has requested the data.

MALWARE

Malware is malicious software written with the intent of compromising a system. These programs can perform a variety of functions some of which include stealing or deleting sensitive data, modifying a system's core functionalities, and secretly tracking the victim's activities.

There are various factors that can lead to the installation of malware in your system. One is running an older or pirated version of an operating system which is not safe or updated, and thus vulnerable to attacks. Clicking on unknown links or installing fake and pirated software, can also lead to downloading malicious programs.

The major types of malware are:

(1). Virus: A program that is capable of infecting software and disabling or modifying a system's core functionality.

(2). Trojans: This type of malware tends to create backdoors in your security to let attackers monitor your activities remotely. It disguises itself as legitimate software or is included in legitimate software that has been tampered with.

(3). Spyware: Hides in the background and tracks everything you do online, including your passwords, credit card numbers, surfing habits, and chats. It can record keystrokes, video you from your webcam and even listen from your microphone.

(4). Keylogger: Specific form of spyware that simply records the keys you type and where you type them. These are then sent to the attacker who can analyze them to find your passwords, chats, credit card numbers and much more.

The best way to avoid these types of malware is to use legitimate antivirus software. Do not download pirated software. Never click on fake antivirus pop-ups that are generated from websites. And always keep your operating system updated.

MOBILE

(1). Malicious Mobile Apps

There is a big misconception that every app available on Google Play Store or the Apple Store is legitimate.

However, this is not the case. Not every app available on these stores is safe for users. Some may contain malicious code that can put your privacy at risk.

The malicious apps may contain a code snippet that can install malware on your device. Besides this, the app may ask for unnecessary permissions that hackers may misuse to extract critical data including your contacts, messages, and media.

Look out for app permissions that request: account access, SMS, microphone access, device admin or contacts, as they can be misused.

Check reviews and ratings. Avoid downloading an app if it has not been downloaded by thousands of people. Do not download apps from third-party app stores. And never download pirated or cracked apps.

(2). Fake Apps with Malware

Hackers often spread malware by designing apps that look identical to popular social media networks, games, and others that are frequently downloaded. In some cases, these apps are advertised via email or text, encouraging you to download what is often indistinguishable from the real thing, but has malicious coding built into the design. Once you download the malicious app, hackers can control your phone and steal your personal information or "ransom" your device until you pay them.

(3). Deceptive QR Barcodes

Today's technology allows us to scan barcodes in order to pay for products or services with our phones. However, cybercriminals have created a series of QR codes that allow them to infiltrate your device through cameras and sensors.

A simple email with a message offering you a good deal on an item or a phishing scheme with a barcode is all it takes to compromise a smartphone.

(4). Public Wi-Fi "Honeypots"

Not all Wi-Fi networks are secure. One popular method used to reel you in is through unsecured wireless internet networks, which you can find in many public places. Scammers use "honeypot" names such as "Airport Wi-Fi" to lure you into their network, paving the way for a cyber-attack.

You can avoid this by turning your Wi-Fi off in public places and using your mobile data plan instead.

INSECURE NETWORKS

Connecting your system or device to an insecure network can allow hackers to gain access to all the files on your system and monitor your activity online. A hacker in control of your system can steal account passwords and even inject malware on authentic websites that you trust.

With programs freely available on the Internet, anyone can sit in a car outside your home and access your critical files, accounting data, usernames and passwords, or any other information on the network.

Connecting to a "free" airport or coffee shop Wi-Fi is dangerous, especially when working on confidential activities online such as banking or accessing company email. These networks are often left unprotected which can allow a malicious hacker in the same shop or region to snoop on you easily.

Never connect to open Wi-Fi networks that you can't trust. Just because it's free, doesn't mean it's safe.

Use strong encryption, like WPA2 on your home and office Wi-Fi router instead of Open or WEP security, as these can easily be hacked.

USB-BASED MALWARE

At the last conference you attended, someone probably handed out free branded USB sticks to keep their business top-of-mind. Hackers will sometimes covertly slip a bunch of infected USB sticks into a company's stash. The instant somebody tries to use one, the computer is taken over by ransomware.

PHYSICAL SECURITY THREATS

These are any threats to your sensitive information that result from other people having direct physical access to your devices like laptops, mobile devices, server rooms, and networking closets. Physical security threats are often underestimated.

Physical threats occur when someone is able to physically gain access to your confidential data, such as data gathered from stolen devices. Physical security breaches can happen at your workplace or even at your home. For example, someone could get hold of your confidential files, on an unattended system, which may not be password protected or does not automatically lock after a period of time.

Be careful how you store confidential information. Use encrypted hard drives, USBs, etc.

Never leave your system unattended. Always protect it with a strong password. Don't leave your phone unlocked and unattended. And make sure proper backup and remote wipe services are enabled in case you lose your device.

Hackers are getting better and better. And the payouts are getting greater and greater. The more technology that is being introduced to our world creates more opportunities for hackers to steal your information.

IN CONCLUSION...

A great way to protect yourself is to stay educated, slow down, read, and partner with a great Technology Provider that stays up-to-date on all the ever-changing technologies.

About Carl

Carl A. Scalzo is the Chief Executive Officer of Online Computers. Since founding the company in 2012, he has built a dedicated team of over 50 employees in three locations. Carl is responsible for the management, development, and strategic direction of the company's technology systems and functions, while maintaining a strong, personal relationship with his clients, as well as his business partners and vendors.

With over 30 years' experience, Carl has assisted his clients in understanding how information technology can aid in furthering the success of their business. He specializes in integrating the most advanced, secure, and reliable technology systems for his clients. Carl has a deep understanding of the importance of business continuity and how to further grow the success of a business or organization strictly through the use of technology.

During his career, Carl has gained experience working with multiple business segments including health care facilities, schools, medical offices, legal offices, and Non-Profit organizations. His business reach extends throughout New York, New Jersey, Maryland, Washington, D.C., and Las Vegas.

With significant experience in the financial fundraising software, Blackbaud CRM, Carl has been responsible for the management of information systems and consulting services for many Non-Profit organizations. He was intimately involved in five of the largest Blackbaud CRM implementations throughout the country, and has been chair of the Finance Technology People Innovation (FTPI) Conference for the Jewish Federations of North America, several times.

Carl is a regular presenter and speaker at conferences and events and was selected to speak on Cybersecurity at New York Law School. He has been featured in newspapers such as The New Jersey Jewish News and has received mentions in a number of volumes and other publications. In addition, Carl has also been published in the Amazon Bestseller, *The Business Owner's Essential Guide to I.T. & All Things Digital.*

CHAPTER 4

YOU ARE THE WEAKEST LINK

THE THREAT THAT USERS POSE TO THEIR NETWORKS

BY TOM CROSSLEY

What we have learned over the last several years is that the number one threat to cybersecurity in your business is not viruses or a breach of your firewall. It's your employees! The biggest threat to cybercrime is the end user. Statistics show that up to 92% of the data loss breaches that happen in a company, ultimately stem from the users inside the network. A percentage of those are due to malicious intent from existing employees (approximately 12%), but the vast majority of these breaches are just obvious, simple missteps that could be avoided.

One of the common behaviors that I routinely train businesses on is that employees should think twice before clicking on an email or even a website. One of the most common attacks is by using phishing emails. Phishing is an email that is trying to get the recipient to click on a link, open a document, or provide information. A typical phishing email asks users to input their credentials to an Office 365 account or to Google. However, what the user is really doing is opening up a link to a bad guy's server and providing their email and company credentials to the bad guy.

THE DANGER OF PHISHING SCHEMES

What's changed over the last couple of years is that we are seeing more and more of these phishing emails targeted to specific people, like the CFO, accountant or office manager, who can control the transference of funds. In the IT world today, companies are getting pretty adept at protecting the perimeter of their network with firewalls, antivirus, and anti-ransomware. The bad guys know this and have shifted tactics. They still want to get into your network and they know your employees are their softest targets for an attack. If a bad guy can get to a user inside your network, they are bypassing all the perimeter security and have a way to get right into the heart of the network itself. Phishing emails are specifically designed to get to the user.

By now most everybody's heard of the old Nigerian prince email. That actually scammed many people at first, but now everybody's pretty much aware of that trick. So the bad guys are getting even more advanced in their attacks. For instance, one example is that they will send a phishing email that looks like it's coming from the IRS or from Microsoft. If they can convince the user to click on a link or open an attachment, they can get access to the entire network.

HOW TO AVOID THE DECEPTION OF SOCIAL ENGINEERING

Lately, we're seeing an increase in two-pronged attacks. The bad guys aren't just being more targeted with their attacks, they're attacking from multiple fronts.

I was talking to one of the local FBI agents in the cybercrime division here in Boston, and he was telling me about a recent incident where the accountant at a company, received an email to his company account. And again, these emails are very targeted, and it basically said, "Here's an overdue invoice from ABC Widget Company. Can you take a look at it?" This accountant didn't recognize the sender and was smart enough to delete it, which was great. But ten minutes later, the accountant got a phone call directly to his desk, and the person on the line said, "Hey, this Mike from ABC Widget Company. Did you get that email I sent with your overdue invoice?" This phone call caused the accountant to question himself. So, he went back and pulled that email out of the trash, and then double-clicked the PDF attachment. In so doing, he unintentionally ransomed every file in the company. It wasn't minutes until the president of the company came out of his office asking why he couldn't open any files.

Emails are coming in that are crafted for the individual and for the specific type of business that the target is in. We're finding that these guys will even do research and approach on social media, like LinkedIn and Facebook.

We had a client who is the CFO at a company, whose wife got a call on her cell phone from a caller who said, "Hi! This is Mike and I'm an old buddy of Bill's from Boston College. [LinkedIn] How's he doing? Does Cathy (their daughter) still play soccer [Facebook]? Hey, does Bill still work at ABC Widget Company [LinkedIn]?" At this point, she was feeling comfortable with "Mike" and they started a "casual" conversation. Without thinking, she gave him valuable information about her husband's position, title, boss, company size, what the company does, etc.

The hacker took that information and crafted a multi-pronged attack on her husband at work. Luckily, the husband was smart enough to see through it. And even though the attacker mentioned his daughter's name and the conversation with his wife, the husband, who was the CFO at his company, realized that this was a malicious attempt and he didn't fall for it. But again, this is just another example of how the bad guys are really working very hard now on these individual attacks.

More and more, these attacks rely heavily on social engineering. It was Sun Tzu who said, "All warfare is based on the art of deception." So we need to remember that this is warfare, and the deception is real. These guys are modern-day con artists. It's just that the modern-day con artist can do it now very anonymously. They don't have to do it face-to-face anymore. And, again, their goal is to get you to click on something, or to influence you to provide them with some information. They do their research to come up with a good enough story to get the user to believe them and comply with whatever they're looking for.

Make no mistake about it, if you look at your business, no matter how big or how small, you have something of value for these hackers. So they will do whatever they can to get that information.

BIG BUSINESS FOR CYBERCRIMINALS

For hackers, this is business. And they have learned and adapted their business model and operating procedures. Two years ago, they were more likely to send out 50,000 generic emails to the masses, hoping that somebody would click on something. But as antivirus and anti-spam technology got better and users (you and your employees) got smarter, these types of emails were no longer as productive or effective for the bad guys. So, they changed their business model. Today, the bad guys research their target and carefully craft their attack for a particular individual.

And believe me, these guys are in business just like you and me. Their profit and loss statements are heavily dependent on their revenue stream – meaning you and your business. And they put a lot of money and effort into working on new, evolving ways to get at your money.

This really is BIG business, it is not small potatoes. Ransomware, as an industry, is a great example of how profitable it is when someone can convince your users to click on the wrong thing. Without cooperative users, the ransomware industry would be nowhere.

Most of these cybercriminals are operating within criminal organizations. Many originate in Eastern Europe and the old Soviet Bloc. An interesting fact about these criminal cyber-organizations is that today they are hiring more sociologists and psychologists than they are programmers. More proof that they are targeting the end users.

Have you ever heard of Evgeniy Bogachev? Probably not. Some consider him to be the father of ransomware. His net worth is estimated to be in excess of 10 Billion dollars. He's thought to be retired on his boat somewhere on the Black Sea. The FBI has posted a three-million-dollar reward for him. He was the first one to really start targeting individuals with social engineering and monetizing that with the use of ransomware.

Even today, the average ransomware syndicate nets $3.4 billion before they get shut down. So this is big business. Even if it's only $300 a whack for home users, when you multiply that by the number of attacks every single day across all business industries, we're talking about serious money. So, these guys are very motivated, patient and diligent at trying to get your information.

Chances are very good that you know someone who has fallen victim to one of these social engineering attacks. But the chance they've admitted it are pretty low. Herein lies one of the challenges to fighting these attacks – very few individuals and even fewer businesses ever report being a victim. Nobody likes to admit to being conned. The FBI estimates that fewer than 10% of businesses report being victimized. From our experience, it's less than that!

WATCH OUT FOR THESE RED FLAGS

Here are some steps you can take to help you protect yourself from these types of targeted threats. First and foremost, be suspicious. Just because you're not paranoid doesn't mean they're not out to get you! When you get a suspicious email, don't just start clicking.

We were involved is a case where it took us months to complete the forensics. We ultimately learned that this company's accountant had been the victim of a targeted phishing attack and had given up his email credentials.

For two months the criminals patiently monitored the email account without the accountant's knowledge. Then they set up rules within the email account that allowed them to start corresponding with the accountant's contacts without their knowledge. At this point, they were free to communicate with all the accountant's email contacts *as if they were the accountant*. And the accountant had no knowledge of the communication.

The criminals started sending messages to the company's suppliers. They even mimicked the communication style of the accountant! Over weeks the criminals patiently told the suppliers that the company would, in the near future, be changing banks. And week after week, they would give just small updates, staying in contact with the suppliers and being very patient. When the time came, they told the suppliers to start sending payments to this new bank account. They even provided a "notarized" document with the new account information. The notarized document was photoshopped from an actual document the accountant had sent out months earlier on an unrelated matter.

The suppliers did as they were told. About two weeks later, the accountant at the company who had been compromised, called the supplier and asked why they hadn't been paid. To which the supplier said, "Of course you've been paid, we sent it to the new account you gave us." That was their first indication that they had been hacked.

BEST PRACTICES FOR PREVENTING A PHISHING SCAM

Other best practices to help you protect yourself online is to be on the alert for anything suspicious, sounds urgent, is trying to get you to bypass typical company procedures, or anyone asking for money. In fact, I recommend that companies require two signatures to release funds in a wire transfer as a safety precaution.

Every company, no matter how big or how small, should be doing security training for their employees and users. Education and awareness are the keys to staying safe. The training that we do typically starts off with a targeted and controlled phishing expedition that is sent out to all the users. We do this to get a baseline of where everyone in that business is at in terms of their awareness. Usually, we find out that anywhere from 30 to 40% of the users will voluntarily give up information that could lead to an attack if it was given to the wrong person. But after cybersecurity awareness training, we see that number go down, usually to less than 5% of the users who would fall for an attack. And we don't just train on email, but with phone calls as well, because that's becoming a more popular scam on the phone.

The basic behaviors to look for in a potential phishing scam include if the email sender or caller has a sense of urgency and they want you to commit an action in a specific timeframe. Another one would be if they insist you do something for them as a favor, especially if it violates company policy. For instance, sometimes hackers will pretend to be co-workers claiming to have lost their passwords and they will ask you to log them in. And some of these attacks are even starting to use artificial intelligence to script these emails, and they are using bots to send them.

Proper training of your employees and other users, and following these best practices, will go a long way in protecting you from many of the cybercrimes in existence today.

About Tom

Tom Crossley is an Information Technology support expert who is passionate about delivering technology that "just plain works the way it's supposed to."

Tom is founder and president of Fairoaks IT, bringing world-class, enterprise-level IT support to small and medium-sized businesses for almost 30 years.

Technology advances at a dizzying speed. While technology helps small-to-medium size companies, it also frightens them as they can't afford the infrastructure to actively adopt the newest and best, nor to defend themselves from the constant threat of being invaded or outdated. For a fraction of the cost, the small-to-medium size company can have all the benefits of a large company's in-house IT-power from Fairoaks. Their motto, *"You Manage Your Business. We'll Manage The Technology Behind It."* sums it all up.

Tom prides himself in providing personal service. Distinguishing themselves from a large IT chain's off-the-shelf service, Fairoaks staff knows their client's business, their names and their unique situations. They enlarge and empower small companies. Tom's ethical stand is, "I treat my client's money as if it was my own." There is no one-size-fits-all service. All his clients' IT needs are crafted to align with their business and their budget. "I have to be creative to give them state-of-the-art, essential and affordable service and I'm proud of it," says Tom. Many business owners are proud to add Fairoaks to their "My doctor, My financial advisor, and My IT guy" list.

It's Tom's firm belief that the success of small-to-medium size companies is the key to strengthening our nation's economy. Because of this, he enjoys sharing his expertise with other business owners speaking on data security, network management, business continuity and other topics at live events, radio broadcasts, and webinars. He's written two books, one of which made Amazon's Best Seller List.

Tom graduated *summa cum laude* from the University of Massachusetts in 1979 with a dual degree in Industrial Engineering and Operations Research, and a minor in Industrial Psychology. Before applying his practical, no-nonsense approach to the IT arena, Tom worked for GE as a consultant and manager throughout the US, the Caribbean and Asia, then co-founded a property management company in Massachusetts.

Tom brings his dedication and focus to his personal interests. He is an avid, instrument-rated private pilot who also has a passion for invention. In 2010, Tom patented a new product for a portable, off-airport aircraft tie-down system, and along with his son, Adam, co-founded Storm Force Tie Downs.

The product has been sold at trade shows and online since 2011.

Away from the office, Tom likes to spend time with his family, getting away to the cabin in Maine for some hiking or snowmobiling.

You can connect with Tom at:

- Tom@FairoaksIT.com
- www.LinkedIn.com/in/TomCrossley

CHAPTER 5

YOUR FIRST LINE OF DEFENSE
FIREWALL AND NETWORK SECURITY PROTECTION

BY HUEY HUYNH

I started in the IT industry almost thirty years ago, and at that time, the Internet was still in its infancy. As time has progressed, the Internet has only continued to get faster and bigger. With that, cybercrime has advanced as well. Now, small businesses that store data online, have websites and email, utilize e-commerce and other file-sharing features, have become prime targets for cybercriminals.

More and more Internet hackers are starting to target small businesses because so many small businesses don't understand the necessary layers of protection they need to protect themselves adequately. It's similar to your home. If you have a lock on your front door, a burglar isn't going to go straight up to the front door and try to pick the lock. If he wants to get in, the burglar will look for an easier entrance point, perhaps an open window, or a back patio door that has been left unlocked. These represent an easier form of entry, rather than just coming in through the front door. It is the same with cybercriminals online. They may not attack your system directly, but instead, look for other ways to access your sensitive information.

YOUR FIREWALL IS YOUR FIRST LINE OF DEFENSE

Your firewall is only the first line of defense for your small business. If you don't have one, then you are more likely leaving yourself open and vulnerable for hackers to break into your system. Many times, we have helped clients implement their firewalls when they didn't have adequate security in place.

One company came to us for help because the hacker had encrypted all of their information and demanded they pay him money to get access back to their files. After some investigation and inspection, we found they did not have a firewall at all, and they used Remote Desktop to allow employees to access their computers remotely. The hackers exploited the vulnerability in the holes in their security to hack into their network. This should never happen to a small business!

Having a firewall in place is essential, because you have to remember that small businesses are not just protecting their own data, but also the information of their clients as well. Many times, small businesses will have sensitive information such as credit card numbers or Social Security numbers on their servers that are left vulnerable to attack. We even found potential clients that have patient medical information, for instance, that they need to protect in dental and doctor's offices.

So having a firewall in place is very important for your small business security, because if you do not have that first line of defense, you are leaving yourself open to being hacked. The costs of being hacked go far beyond just the ransom fee to retrieve your encrypted files. Additionally, there's the cost of lost productivity, employee downtime, potential fines from the government or other regulatory agencies, and perhaps worst of all, a damaged reputation.

TAKING YOUR FIREWALL TO THE NEXT-GEN

A lot of small businesses, and especially those that are just starting out, have the misconception that when they get the Internet and a router from their ISP, they are automatically protected. While the Internet provider will give them a router, the firewall that comes with it is not a true firewall. Rather, it is more the equivalent to what firewalls were twenty-five years ago in terms of technology. These outdated firewalls usually only do what is called port blocking.

Back in the days when browsing the Internet using a web browser was safe, these old firewalls would block out the ports that were not being used, and that was about it. But now, hackers utilize updated technology and can embed viruses and malware directly into the websites. So port blocking itself is no longer very helpful because so many hackers utilize the web to inject malicious codes and infect the network with malware using the same port the web browser uses. So you need to have the next-gen firewall that will actually block out the malicious web pages. Moreover, these next-gen firewalls will look at the information that flows through websites and identify if one is a threat. So for new businesses starting out, just because you have the Internet and a router does not mean you have adequate protection.

Also, I would recommend buying a commercial grade, rather than a home-grade firewall because so many of the home-grade firewalls only do the same thing that the Internet providers do. So it's not very useful. That's why you need the commercial grade.

Ideally, small businesses are going to want to look for a firewall that has the built-in antivirus protection, anti-spyware protection, and what is called IPS or intruder prevention service protection. It would be good also to have a deep packet inspection, and this is for looking at information on the web page, and finding the signature threat and blocking it.

If you want to go a step further to protect the information flowing in and out of your system, then you will want to get a firewall that has a content filter as well. This will prevent the information from not only flowing out, but it also protects the users from going to dangerous sites.

PROTECTING CPA FIRMS WITH INTERNET SECURITY

We have small business clients from all across the spectrum, but we do specialize in CPA firms. We have been working with CPA firms for over twenty years now and continue to work very closely with many CPA firms. Moreover, this is timely, because recently, CPA firms have become more and more of a target by cybercriminals. Also, this makes sense because CPA firms have a lot of Social Security information from their clients. So, if a hacker breaks into a CPA firm, they can potentially get hundreds and hundreds of pieces of sensitive client contact information that the CPA firm has on file.

So this is of paramount concern for CPA firms because, in addition to the customer fallout, the resulting fines by the government can be too much for a small firm to bear. I've even seen it when these fines have put the small CPA firms out of business. And many CPA firms, especially smaller ones, just don't have the technical know-how to implement strong firewall protection.

We have a fully-staffed help desk team, local to Kansas City, in order to support our clients. Our technicians begin working on client solutions within three minutes of receiving a client request, guaranteed. And during the busy season for CPAs, from the first of the year until the end of April, our help desk is available 24/7 so that they're not slowed down in any way while they're doing their CPA work. We also ensure our staff is trained and maintain certifications for the products we support. These certifications help our clients know that we follow protocol and we're conducting our service by the book. Some equipment even required certifications before working on them.

STEPS TO NETWORK SUCCESS

As for the six steps to success, the first thing would be to ensure that you have a next-gen firewall that can protect your network. Secondly, the firmware on the firewall needs to be up-to-date. The firmware on a firewall needs to be updated just like the antivirus on your computer does. This patches any security holes or other bugs a hacker may seek to exploit. Similarly, any other equipment and software need to be regularly updated. This can be handled by your IT staff or an outsourced IT company like ours. Your firewall can detect and stop incoming threats through the Internet, so having up to date hardware and firmware is very important.

The third thing to do is to make sure that if you have a website on your network, or any service provided to users on the public internet, it needs to be separated from other devices on your network like your computers and servers. Services like a website are the most reachable by hackers. That's why you need to harden your defenses to withstand constant attack. This can be done through a "DMZ", or demilitarized zone, which is a function in any good commercial grade firewall. If a hacker tries to use your website as a foothold, he will not be able to penetrate through to your network.

The fourth thing would be to review all of the rules in the firewall to ensure that the rules are up to date, and they are not allowing more than what they need in order to keep the network and your staff up and running. Also, review the rules that don't map out to make sure certain things don't get out, and make sure that the content filter is enabled, so that it will defend the internal users from going to any potentially harmful sites. Some firewalls even give you the ability to stop access from countries that are known to be threatening, like Russia or China, so unless you have a business that deals with those countries, it's a good idea not to allow access to and from them.

The fifth thing is to make sure you have antivirus and antispyware (they also are called Endpoint protection.) Having layers of defense better protects your network. Have your IT provider routinely check to ensure your Endpoint security is up-to-date and adequately protecting your network.

The sixth thing is to make sure all computers on your network are patched and have the latest software installed. This to ensure all vulnerabilities and security holes are plugged, so hackers can't exploit those security holes. Make sure your IT provider continuously monitors your computers and network for security holes. They should be able to report to you if there are any vulnerabilities in your network.

IGNORANCE IS NOT BLISS

We have helped numerous companies that have fallen victim to ransomware after the fact, and we have helped them recover from it. We will go in and redo their firewall and inspect the rules that open up too much access to the Internet. A lot of people don't realize this, but they will often open up what's called a terminal desktop or terminal service, so that they can remote in from the outside to the computer. While this is very convenient for workers, it's something hackers look for first, and is often the reason companies suffer a cyber-attack in the first place.

Hackers will use a bot to scan the Internet for terminal desktops. If your password is not strong enough, hackers can eventually guess it and hack into your computer and get access to your network or whatever they want. They can even install spyware in your computer so that when the victim accesses their bank account, the hacker can watch it and steal that information. Hackers can use that terminal computer to access accounting software like QuickBooks and scan for credit card information, all totally undetected within your network.

Unfortunately, we see breaches happen all the time. Some

companies do not protect their data and unfortunately, they are hacked into. We've seen small business held up by various ransomware and then have that data totally lost in the attack. Furthermore, sometimes that critical information can be sold to others on the dark web and the data is used for criminal purposes.

So it's not just with the major companies, like the big stores and other large online retailers, but also many small businesses are hacked regularly. So I want to keep spreading the word out there that small businesses are the number one target. If a large company with a big budget for IT can be hacked, small businesses are like low-hanging fruit for hackers. You have to protect yourself from these threats.

My goal is to bring more awareness to small businesses, and especially CPA firms, that they need to use a firewall on their network. We were honored to receive the MSP 500, and the Tech Elite 250 in both 2017 and 2018. The MSP500 recognizes the top 500 Managed Service Providers in the nation, and the Tech Elite 250 is an award for certifications to technician ratio.

When it comes to network and data security, this is a case of where being ignorant about the subject may actually be harmful to you. So hopefully this book will be able to help educate you on this need, and spread the word on ways to help you protect your network. Again, this is not just for your own good in your business, but also for protecting your client's information as well.

About Huey

Huey Huynh helps his clients leverage technologies to run their businesses efficiently and protect them from hackers and disasters. Having immigrated from Vietnam when he was in high school, he used his strong work ethic and became the first in his family to get a Bachelor's degree. After graduating, he found he had the talent for technology and began working in the IT industry in 1991.

During this time, he helped many enterprise-level companies utilize technology to run more efficiently and securely. It dawned on him that small businesses were not benefitting from these technologies for a few reasons: lack of expertise, lack of funds, and lack of knowledge. In 2005, Huey entered the small business world to help small business owners and he hasn't looked back since.

Huey started his company with the philosophy of helping others. That's why he puts a strong emphasis on education for his team, clients, and colleagues. He shares his knowledge through various media including a print newsletter, email alerts, and webinars. His hope is to educate as many people as possible to ensure everyone is safe from cyber threats and can run their businesses without technology issues. Huey's clientele span the entire business map and range from non-profits to rapidly expanding national companies.

Huey and his team's dedication to serving Kansas City businesses led the company to win the CRN MSP 500 and CRN Tech Elite 250 two years in a row. Huey and his team are constantly following industry trends and tweaking the business to provide the best service possible to Kansas City businesses.

You can connect with Huey at:

- www.KansasCityITconsulting.com
- 913-228-1245
- ask@bdsNOW.com

CHAPTER 6

DISCOVER THE 21 MOST CRITICAL I.T. SECURITY PROTECTIONS

BY RANDY BANKOFIER

IN THE NEXT 7 MINUTES:

Discover the
21 MOST CRITICAL I.T. SECURITY PROTECTIONS
that Protect your Business from Cyber Criminals

It was just another busy day at the office, and I had a few minutes to check my email. And there it was, a personal invitation to meet with our local FBI agent, a Secret Service agent, City of Portland, Oregon officials and about a dozen other IT professionals (mostly from county governments and large IT departments) to discuss something I've been very passionate about for almost a decade... how to protect local business computer networks in Portland from cybercriminals, hackers and data breaches.

MY MEETING WITH THE FBI, SECRET SERVICE AND CITY OF PORTLAND

I jumped at the chance. I've been studying cyber-crime since 2007 and I wanted to make sure I was staying abreast of any and all new developments. My goal has always been to employ the absolute best and most affordable protections possible to better protect my own businesses, but more importantly, the over 700 IT business clients we've been serving since 2001 in Portland, throughout the US, and as far as the United Kingdom and Japan.

The requirements for attending the FBI's meeting was that no audio/video recordings were allowed, plus we must not leak any confidential information of the local cases discussed. But, there's still so much I can share and that's why I'm writing to you today.

WHO ARE CYBER CRIMINALS #1 TARGET? WELL, THAT'D BE YOU

Every single day, I seem to meet a business owner who thinks they're safe from cybercrime. "We're too small," they say or "I'll take my chances."

Did you know this is exactly why small businesses with 5 to 100 employees are the #1 target for cybercriminals? Cybercriminals know that the bank accounts at these businesses are managed by regular people and these regular people are no match for organized cyber gangs.

DID YOU KNOW?

- 1 in 5 small businesses will suffer a cyber-breach this year.
- 81% of all breaches happen to small and medium-sized businesses.
- 97% of breaches could have been prevented with today's technology.

HOW DO CYBER CRIMINALS MAKE MONEY?

Cybercriminals don't do this for fun. The old days of some 16-year-old pimply teenage kid creating computer viruses to delete your data, show dirty pop-up messages on your screen or just crash your PC so hard that it won't ever start again are pretty much over. Today you're now up against sophisticated cyber-criminal organizations making hundreds of millions of dollars every year.

During my meeting with the FBI, Secret Service and the City of Portland, the FBI Agent actually taught all of us how to start our own ransomware business that makes $2 Million a Year and he did all this in about 5-10 minutes. Is that crazy or what? It's easy to understand why cybercriminals are now creating over 80,000 new pieces of malware every single day!

#1 MONEYMAKER - RANSOMWARE

Ransomware is currently the biggest money maker, followed by spear phishing attacks that directly target business owners and staff who have access to the business's bank accounts.

Nowadays, you've either been hit with ransomware or you know somebody that has. Basically, it goes like this.

1. A business computer falls victim to ransomware.
2. The ransomware encrypts all the data it finds. This includes data on your servers, PC's and laptops, even remote Google drives and Microsoft OneDrive, your backups... basically everything. It will search for and locate everything that the victimized computer has access to and then it encrypts all that data.
3. You'll receive a Ransom Note (i.e. Popup message on your computer screen). The note will demand payment in the hundreds, thousands or even millions of dollars. For example, a hospital in Hollywood California received a ransom note for $17 million dollars. Their entire hospital was down for a whole week, and the hospital's backups were unusable, so they had to settle with the criminals.
4. Your ransom payment must be made using Bitcoin or other designated electronic currencies. These types of currencies are basically untraceable.

5. If you don't pay within 24-48 hours, then the ransom doubles.

6. If you don't pay within 72 hours, the decryption key is deleted. At this point there's no way the criminals can recover your data.

7. If you do pay the ransom before the deadline, then in almost all cases, you'll actually receive your data back. The criminals figure that if you didn't get your data, then word would get around and nobody would pay.

8. But, if you do pay, they target you over and over. So, you're screwed either way.

Check out: www.KrebsOnSecurity.com for 36 more ways cyber-criminals make money off hacking one of your business's computers.

WHEN YOU FALL VICTIM TO A CYBER-ATTACK THROUGH NO FAULT OF YOUR OWN, WILL THEY CALL YOU STUPID...OR JUST IRRESPONSIBLE?

It's EXTREMELY unfair, isn't it? Victims of all other crimes – burglary, rape, mugging, carjacking, theft – get sympathy from others. They are called "victims" and support comes flooding in, as it should.

But if your business is the victim of a cybercrime attack where client, employee or patient data is compromised, you will NOT get much sympathy. You will be instantly labeled as stupid or irresponsible. You will be investigated and questioned about what you did to prevent this from happening – and if the answer is not adequate, you can be found liable, facing serious fines and lawsuits EVEN IF you trusted an outsourced IT support company to protect you.

This is why you need to arm yourself with the following must-have knowledge.

21 Most Critical I.T. Security Protections Your Business Needs Immediately

I have no magic wand and there's no magic pill either. As a matter of fact, there's no one security protection that solves all your cyber-security problems. If there were, I'd be the first to tell you about it and insist that you purchase it as fast as possible. But there's not.

Since there's no one solution, here's my list of 21 must-have critical protections you absolutely need to have for your business. This has taken me years of study, research and analysis and I want to give the FBI, Secret Service and City of Portland officials a big thank you for their presentations and Q&A session. They helped me solidify my list below.

1. *Security Assessment*
   You can't make management decisions if you're not regularly assessing where you're at. Therefore, you need to establish a baseline, close vulnerabilities and perform periodic assessments.

2. *Backups*
   Backup local. Back to the cloud. Have an offline backup for each month of the year. Perform test restores of your backups monthly.

3. *Next Generation Firewall*
   A firewall separates your business computer network from the bad guys out on the internet and not all firewalls are the same. Your cable provider's firewall is not acceptable! Your firewall needs a Comprehensive Security Subscription, including an Intrusion Prevention System, and that subscription must be actively licensed at all times to help stop over 80,000 new attacks developed every single day. That's over 29 million a year!

4. *Advanced Endpoint Security*

During my meeting, the FBI agent reported that anti-virus software is 9% effective against today's threats, so we must use Advanced Endpoint Security. This latest technology replaces outdated anti-virus technology and protects against file-less and script-based threats and can even rollback a ransomware attack.

5. *Computer Security Updates*

Subscribe to an automated "critical update" service to keep the operating systems of your PCs, laptops and servers constantly updated with the latest security updates and patches to minimize risks from security threats and attacks targeting known bugs and security vulnerabilities.

6. *3rd Party Software Patching*

Subscribe to an automated "critical update" service to keep common software applications that are found on most computers constantly updated. Ones like Adobe Flash, Adobe Reader, Shockwave, iTunes, QuickTime, Safari, Google Chrome, Skype, Firefox, Java and more.

7. *Network Security Policies*

Apply security policies on your network. Examples: Deny or limit USB file storage access, enable enhanced password policies, set user screen timeouts, limit user access, enforce encryption and especially harden your servers, so they're less vulnerable to attack.

8. *Advanced Email Security*

Most cyber-attacks originate in your email, so subscribe to a security service that scans every email to help protect against payload and phishing attacks, blocks and reduces spam and provides the ability to send encrypted emails. Having Office 365 or G-Suite/Gmail are not enough.

9. *Advanced Web Browsing Security*

The 2nd most common cyber-attack method is through your staff's web browsing, so make sure to subscribe to a service that can block malicious destinations and activity before a connection is ever established, even when users are working remotely.

10. *Advanced Internet DNS*

Did you know that your competitor can go on the Dark Web and pay about $20 to take down your website using a DDoS attack? At that instant, the cybercriminal's fleet of millions of victimized computers across the world will start sending so much information to your web server that your website will literally go off-line, never to be seen again until the attack is thwarted or canceled. With Advanced Internet DNS your website can withstand these attacks.

11. *Employee Security Awareness Training*

During my meeting, the FBI's #1 recommendation, even above firewalls & endpoint security, is for business owners to train their employees – and train them often! Teach them about data security, email attacks, and your policies and procedures. Do this by subscribing to a reliable and proven "done for you" web-based video training solution that includes automated fake attacks that are sent to your staff. If your employee clicks on the wrong thing, they'll receive instant remedial training and you'll be notified via weekly management reports.

12. *Dark Web Monitoring*

Would you want to know if your username and password, or your staff's login credentials, or your banking login info, or your customer data or your employees' personal identifiable information (i.e., PII) were suddenly listed for sale on the Dark Web? Of course you would! Subscribe to a reliable monitoring service that can alert you immediately if your information goes up for sale on the Dark Web, so you can be proactive in preventing a data breach.

13. *Multi-Factor Authentication*

Utilize Multi-Factor Authentication whenever you can including on your network, banking websites and even social media. It adds an additional layer of protection to ensure that even if your password does get stolen, your data stays protected.

14. *Password Management*

Where do you and your staff currently store usernames and passwords to all your computer systems and websites? Stop wrestling with sticky notes and spreadsheets and start using a real system designed for an organization like yours. Subscribe to a service where you can organize, share and audit all the important passwords and password-related tasks handled within your organization.

15. *Local Network-Layer Vulnerability Scan*

Use a network layer VA scanner to identify security risks on every system plugged into your computer network (i.e., PC's, servers, VoIP phones, wireless access points, firewalls, switches, printers, security cameras). Identify rogue systems that haven't been accounted for and identify new risks that have been discovered or introduced. Great VA scanning software starts around $11,000 and requires a trained team to operate. It's best to subscribe to an automated service, but make sure it detects a minimum of 45,000 exploits.

16. *SIEM Monitoring*

This type of monitoring helps identify if a cyber-criminal has got their "foot in the door" and is actively trying to access your data or trying to make further changes to your network security, so they can gain even more control. Marriott Hotel disclosed a four-year-long breach involving personal and financial information of 500 million guests at its Starwood properties. I recommend SIEM Monitoring to help identify breaches sooner, before you're front-page news.

17. *$2,500 of Bitcoin*

If it's your first time, sometimes it can take up to a week to acquire Bitcoin or other electronic currencies. The last thing you want to do is try to acquire it when you're under attack and your data is being held for ransom because if you can't pay in 72 hours, then your data is gone forever.

18. *Cyber Insurance Policy*

If all else fails, protect your income and business with cyber-crime, cyber damage and recovery insurance policies. But watch out for exclusion and limitation clauses! I wish I had a dollar for every small business owner that told me they don't have to worry about all the IT security measures I was recommending because they had cyber insurance.

You should see their faces when I ask to see their policy and point out all the exclusions and limitations. Yes, the fine print is important, so make sure to read it. Let me share the process.

When you make a claim against your cyber insurance policy, the insurance carrier is going to have a specialized IT team review your entire network. The first sign they find that you're not living up to the terms of the policy, they will deny your claim.

They'll do everything they can to find that you've violated an exclusion clause. If your firewall doesn't have intrusion prevention, if your computers don't have security patches applied within 3 days, if the firmware on network devices aren't up-to-date, if test restores of backups aren't done every quarter, if old hard drives aren't properly wiped, if laptops aren't encrypted, if there's no SIEM monitoring, then they'll DENY YOUR CLAIM.

So make sure you have an expert review your Cyber Insurance Policy and make sure your IT team is following its terms.

19. *Mobile Device Management*
   If you're providing company-owned smartphones and/or tablets to employees, then it's critical to protect their data, enforce company policies, configure allowed apps, remotely locate and wipe stolen devices, etc.

20. *Full Disk Encryption*
   Whenever possible, the goal is to encrypt files at rest, in motion (think email) and especially on mobile devices. Mobile devices get lost and are easy to steal, so make sure each has full disk encryption.

21. *Business Continuity Plan*
   No one can predict the future; however, are you ready with a sound business continuity plan and backup processes in the event of a cyber-attack, fire or other impending disaster?

HOW CAN YOU EASILY IMPLEMENT ALL 21 SECURITY PROTECTIONS?

Does all this sound complicated? It doesn't have to be, but if you're a Do-It-Yourself kind of business owner, I've got some discouraging news. This stuff is expensive and complicated. It's taken me years to not only identify these security protections, but to also hire and develop a highly-trained IT team that can implement them.

So, what can a successful, busy business owner do?

I suggest hiring a competent outsourced IT provider that is:

1. Trained in all 21 Security Protections and
2. Offering all 21 on a subscription basis in an affordable monthly package.

About Randy

Randy Bankofier has been providing IT support and IT solutions to over 700 small to mid-sized businesses since 2001. Randy is most proud of his company's Annual Client Retention Rate of nearly 95% during the last six years.

He believes so much in what his company does that he backs it up with their No-Risk 100% Money-Back Guarantee. If for any reason a client is dissatisfied, unhappy or just changes their mind, they let Randy know within 60-days and his team will put everything back the way it was and reimburse 100% of their money. His clients have absolutely ZERO risk for trying his company out.

Randy's best known for his "Famous 7 Guarantees":

1. FREE VoIP Phone System – GUARANTEED
2. Help in 7 Minutes – GUARANTEED
3. Never Lose Your Data – GUARANTEED
4. Your Absolute Satisfaction or Money Back – GUARANTEED.
5. Never Pay the Ransom – GUARANTEED
6. No Vague Invoices – GUARANTEED
7. IT Support Available Around the Clock – GUARANTEED

Randy uses the Topgrading hiring method developed by Dr. Brad Smart to ensure he hires top-notch employees. He believes that his company's culture is created by attracting great people who effortlessly live his core values and deliver their brand promise, which is to: "Help small businesses utilize technology to make their lives easier, their business more competitive and profitable, and to help safeguard what they have worked so hard to attain."

Randy is the author of two other books, *Hassle-Free Computer Support* and *Windows 7 Professional: The Little Black Book.* In 2013 he hosted his own radio program on 1410 AM, "The Money Station" teaching business owners about cloud computing.

Randy graduated from Portland State University with a B.S. in Computer Science and a B.S. degree in Business Administration. He's spent the last 30 years in the IT industry specializing first in software development, then in IT management, IT consulting, cloud computing and IT cybersecurity.

Randy lives in Portland, Oregon with his wife, and is father to three adult boys and one daughter. He enjoys living part of the year in Hawaii enjoying the sun, hiking, snorkeling, sailing, scuba diving and watching his daughter play Division II basketball in Honolulu.

You can connect with Randy at:

- 503-343-4541
- randy@24x7it.com
- https://linkedin.com/in/randybankofier/
- https://24x7it.com

CHAPTER 7

HOW TO QUICKLY AND EFFECTIVELY RESPOND TO AN IT BREACH

YOUR RESPONSE IS JUST AS CRITICAL AS PREVENTION

BY SEAN CONNERY

Every year, the US government and large enterprises alike, spend hundreds of millions of dollars on IT security. Still yet, every single day there are organizations that have their data breached. In fact, based on my research of the Clark School study at the University of Maryland, statistics show that there is a hacking attack every thirty-nine seconds.

Expectations are changing as the frequency and severity of cyber-attacks continue to increase. Based on the accelerating frequency and growing costs of security breaches, Cybersecurity Ventures predicts $6 trillion annually in cybercrime damage by 2021!

Additionally, in their paper, *"Are You Prepared to Respond to a Cyber Attack?"* published by Continuum Managed Services Holdco, LLC, the authors report that 43% of cyber-attacks are targeted towards small business. They go on to say that

64% of companies have experienced web-based attacks, and 62% of businesses have experienced either phishing or social engineering attacks. Furthermore, 59% of companies have experienced a malicious code or botnets, and 51% of businesses have experienced a denial of service attack.

Even organizations with highly sophisticated cyber defense solutions can fall victim to an attack. Businesses should be judged based on how well they manage and respond to an incident, rather than by whether or not they can prevent one from occurring in the first place. However, the most well-protected businesses will be the ones that can focus on both strategies of prevention and response.

So far, this book has presented several great ideas on how you can best protect your company's computer environment against these attacks. But now, my chapter will inform you of the critical steps you need to take in the unfortunate event that you will have to respond to an IT breach.

PREPARE BEFORE AN ATTACK

Athletes do it. Sports teams do it. Airline pilots do it. Professional speakers do it. Musicians do it. Wedding planners do it, heck it's in their title. As the saying goes, "Failing to plan is planning to fail." And it makes sense. If you don't have a plan in place before tragedy hits, you may end up just being frozen in shock. People often panic when they don't have a plan. So proper preparation is the first step in mitigating a cyber attack.

Being prepared for a cybersecurity attack can reduce the risk your business faces and may minimize the potential damages associated with being a victim of an attack. Additionally, planning ahead of time helps to ease the difficulty of managing the response and recovery times.

Planning leads to awareness and preparation leads to readiness.

So part of adequately preparing is to have an established communication plan. This is a communication plan for your contact with outside parties. Depending on the scope of the incident, the response team may need to communicate with outside organizations such as:

- Internet Service Provider's, or ISP's
- Other Incident Response Teams
- Software and Hardware Vendors
- Legal Counsel and Insurance
- The Local News Media
- Law Enforcement

Any communication plan to be used with outside parties should document who is authorized to communicate with each type of outside party and what can and cannot be shared, as well as suggestions on when you should hire an outside communication management company and/or legal company for representation.

Additionally, your communication plan should list out the required staff training and processes for handling the media if and when necessary, and stress the importance of not revealing sensitive information. Having a clear outline on how to handle contact, communication, and other interactions with authorized team members is important.

Doing so will maintain that the released statement is the current status of an incident so that all interactions are up-to-date and consistent. As you can see, this communication plan is multifaceted and involves several potential organizations. So the key is to develop this plan and strategy before you need it.

Other forms of adequate preparation include instituting a solid documentation of the environment, regularly testing a backup system, and training users on cybercrime awareness, just to state a few.

Another good way to plan for an attack is to familiarize yourself with common attack vectors such as removable and external media, attrition through brute force methods, web surfing, email usage, theft, impersonation, and the improper usage or violation of acceptable policies. These best practices are key in documenting the responses to new and unknown threats online.

RESPONDING TO A CRISIS DURING AN ATTACK

The first step is to confirm whether a reported ransomware infection is an actual infection. There are cases where a user reports what they think is ransomware, but it turns out to be adware, phishing, or some other virus. Validation is important because it keeps efforts focused on the important issues. But if you see a ransomware note demanding payment to unlock files, and your system or files are locked or frozen, then you've been hit by an attacker.

Step 1: Confirm

After you have confirmed the reported incident, begin a response by declaring an incident, assembling the response team, and ultimately, take action. Call your organization's insurance company. They will explain their requirements and outline any steps that may need to be taken to protect forensic data or evidence. You will want to support, not hinder, your company's ability to collect on an insurance claim. Review your organizations business continuity or disaster recovery plan, as there may be specific requirements and action items mandated by certain policies.

Business owners should also communicate, or reiterate, the company's rules of disclosure to its employees, and to address what should or should not be communicated via public channels like social media, the press, and with clients. A standard recommendation is that nothing is permitted to be disclosed until the company releases a formal statement, generally after the facts of the event have been gathered and properly analyzed.

During this process, be sure to backup up everything – even on encrypted or infected computers – to create a recovery path if the containment or remediation steps destroy data, or in the event that decryption fails and a recovery key is discovered after the event has occurred. There are cases where law enforcement releases decryption keys months after an attack has stopped.

Step 2: Containment

For containment, start by running a vulnerability scan, like Nessus, or NMAP/ZENMAP from the Internet against your firewall, looking for anything unusual that shouldn't be open. Then deny all international traffic in the firewall and deny all inbound traffic across your Remote Desktop Protocol, or other remote access tools to your network.

If necessary, enable VPN access first, then RDP across the VPN-protected connection. If possible, unplug your Internet connection at the router and firewall until you have regained control of the network. You can also unplug all switches on the network to help avoid lateral movement of the threat and isolate segments of the network as you work to contain the threat.

Next, you should check all of your security and system logs for any unusual activity. If you have a service to search the Dark Web for stolen credentials, like ID Agent or Spycloud, then you should do that then.

Check your local and domain account for any changes or new accounts you weren't expecting to see. Remove or disable any old accounts and verify new ones created recently. As being expected, new accounts might be relative in that the FBI estimates that most business will take up to nine months to detect a breach in their network.

If not already in place, consider adding OpenDNS for DNS protection to prevent further command and control calls to infected websites and the bot network.

Leverage SentinelOne to help hunt for and isolate the threat, provide additional visibility, and help prevent further spread of the attack. Also, leverage a Security Information Event Manager, like EventTracker, to analyze and provide additional visibility into the activity going through the firewall, in Active Directory, and endpoints.

Finally, be sure to receive authorization in writing or email from your insurance provider before moving on to the next steps.

Step 3: Remediation

Before beginning these steps, unplug the Internet connection and either unplug the switches on the network or disconnect all computers, including your servers. Consider also removing the gateway IP address from DNS temporarily.

Then clean the domain controller, if possible in safe mode, of the infection. Disable Autorun on all systems on the network using the Group Policy Object in Windows. It is strongly recommended to disable the Autorun feature using Group Policy from the Domain Controller.

Next, disable Windows Task Scheduler on all systems on the network. Likewise, it is strongly recommended to disable the Windows Task Scheduler using Group Policy from the Domain Controller.

Then reset all user passwords to a default password, and share that new password verbally around the office so users can reset their passwords. Do not email it out, and be sure to force users to change from the new temporary password you set. If you only force password changes, then there is a chance the threat actor will reset their compromised account and still have access to the network.

Reset all device passwords, including switches, routers, firewalls, VPNs, and IDS devices. Bring up one server at a time, clean it, and if it's not a required server shut it down until you have completed cleanup of the network. Bring up one workstation at a time, on the network, and clean as needed. Reboot several times looking for a return of the infection. Then check your backups again. Remember, you can never have enough good backups.

Step 4: Recovery

Only restore from clean backups. If clean backups do not exist, I cannot advise as to whether or not to pay the ransom. For some organizations, such as hospitals, the decision to pay ransomware is a life-or-death decision. For others, refusing to pay cybercriminals to unlock the encrypted data could result in millions of dollars lost, or worse.

The FBI has issued a statement, recommending that victims not pay the ransom and backup their files instead. That being said, the FBI's assistant special agent in charge of Cyber Intelligence Program, Joseph Bonavolonta, in a talk at the October 2017 Cyber Security Summit in Boston, suggested that in a majority of cases, companies that fall victim to ransomware attacks cannot recover their files, and he has recommended them to pay the ransom to regain access to their data. So really, this decision is entirely up to the insurance company or business owner.

Then scan your network one more time with relevant tools, such as SentinelOne, Hitman Pro, or other updated security scanning engine. Once the network is back up online, run a new backup job and backup all critical data before allowing users back onto the network. In some instances, this may be a time-consuming effort, but it is well worth it, especially when compared to running the risk of a second or repeat infection occurring.

Step 5: Debrief

The final step is to review and document the entire incident. Work to design and implement a security plan designed for your budget that will help defend against this type of attack in the future.

MEDIA AND PR RESPONSE AFTER AN ATTACK

In addition to the significant costs and risks associated with having a security incident, the potential damage to brand and reputation, and the loss of customer trust, can be equally damaging. Beyond reputation impact, poorly managed and communicated security incidents can affect employee morale, as well as lead to regulatory pressure and or litigation.

The reality is that the reporter's priorities are to the reporter, the editor, rival reporters, and readers or views watching and listening in their audience. The last priority is you, as the source. So it is essential to know what to say, what not to say, and how to say, what information you do provide.

Before speaking with the media, a spokesperson needs to be well prepared and fully understand the angle. That way they know why the interview is important to the reporter and to their readers.

Realize how the printed story may impact your company and stakeholders alike. Finally, make sure that your company's image and position consistently comes through during every interview.

About Sean

Sean Connery is a best-selling author, an international speaker, and a co-founder and president of both Orbis Solutions and ITIS Compliance.

Orbis Solutions, Inc (OSI) is a virtual IT Department that focuses on helping businesses increase their productivity, profitability, and cyber security. OSI provides all the support and services that you would expect from a large in-house IT department, but at a fraction of the cost.

ITIS Compliance is dedicated to conducting and defending PCI and HIPAA audits, as well as other compliance needs. Staffed with certified testers including a CISSP (Certified Information Security Systems Professional) and a CEH (Certified Ethical Hacker), the seasoned penetration testing team methodically investigates systems for potential vulnerabilities and provides solutions for any weaknesses they identify.

Sean's last book, *Under Attack: How to Protect your Business & Bank Account From Fast-Growing, Ultra-Motivated and Highly Dangerous Cybercriminal Rings* was an Amazon Best-Seller in several categories including Network Security and Security & Encryption.

In 2018, Sean was a finalist for the Top Tech Exec Awards in Las Vegas, NV. An award meant to honor those in the community who have an innovative vision and are willing to take risks, in order to make their organizations more successful and productive.

As a Thought Leader in Cyber Security, he has spoken at Microsoft, Harvard, and various other venues to several C-Level Executives across the nation. He keeps business leaders informed about the growing threat of cybercrime and helps them understand what they can do to keep their information safe.

After working in the IT industry for over 25 years and valuing continuing education for both himself and his employees, Sean has amassed several acronyms behind his name. Some of the highlights are CISSP, MCSE (Microsoft Certified Systems Engineer), ITIL (Information Technology Infrastructure Library), VCP (VMware Certified Professional, and CSSP (Certified SonicWALL Security Professional).

Sean's experience and ingenuity enables him to continue growing both OSI and ITIS Compliance, while still being able to make sure his clients receive a level of service that exceeds their expectations. Sean and OSI were honored to be presented with Community Partner of the Year from Positively Kids, a Southern Nevada Charity working to make healthcare accessible to at risk children.

To learn more about Sean Connery:

- Call: 702.979.1861
- Email sean.connery@orbissolutionsinc.com
- LinkedIn at: linkedin.com/in/sconnery
- www.OrbisSolutionsInc.com/Seans-Story/.

CHAPTER 8

UNHACKABLE
AUGMENTED REAL-TIME SECURITY

BY GEORGE MANSOUR

Are you prepared for the CyberWorld?

How do we keep our privacy and security when everything online is being exposed and logged? How do we secure our connections, permissions, and access to sensitive data in an unstable environment? The question is a concern for everyone around the world. Our data information is continuously being tracked and stored.

If you are like the many others I help, then you may also be alarmed about the growing web of technology surrounding us. Although, the real question is, how do we best protect ourselves against these technological innovations?

We must first remember that technology is only a tool. As with any instrument, the operator must take great caution when using the device for privacy and security reasons. We are in danger of allowing the tool an unnecessary amount of control over our lives. Therefore, we need to re-balance our relationship with technology. Education of the digital landscape and the human experience must be administered.

ON THE WEB, BUT NOT OF THE WEB

The Internet is constantly being tweaked and altered to monitor online behavior. These modifications follow surfing habits that model specific tastes while gaining insight into opinions. Therefore, it only shows what you want to see.

Have you ever stopped to consider how much consumerism and convenience is really costing us? We have become intertwined in the web of cyberspace; it is slowly reprogramming our thought process to an involuntary unconscious state of mind. Is this why we created technology?

It is time to liberate ourselves. The Unhackable paradigm shift is a process that enables a balance between new technology and the existing human condition. We can be on the web but not of the web. Unhackable brings forth a school of thought to unravel the complicated nature of the Internet. The digital transformation is not just about technology, but how to create a viable partnership.

The development of technology cannot be stopped, but users can change the way they deal with advancing innovations. Are you ready to take the challenge? Privacy and Security are the two main goals of protecting our sensitive data.

FREEDOM AND THE WEB

As the internet celebrates the 30th anniversary we must ask ourselves as responsible users, are we doing everything in our power to understand this new environment? The innovation has granted incredible access to information that previous generations could have only imagined. In respective analysis, a comparable analogy would be an ocean. Could you traverse a sailboat across the sea without a proper manifesto?

Unhackable provides an anchor that allows users to securely protect their sensitive data. The rapid involvement forced society to adapt in an uncontrolled fashion; leaving users unequipped to process the vast amounts of information-sharing over the medium of the internet found on the web.

A FORMULA FOR FREEDOM

Unhackable was created to build a bridge across the treacherous ocean of the Internet. It provides a methodology that frees its users from the stickiness of the world wide web. We can once again gain a sense of autonomy with the advancing technology in society.

The concept is a timeless solution to carry us through the landscapes of our digital age. Harmony will be restored with our connections to media influences.

The Internet impacts every area of daily life. The result brings forth the knowledge to navigate technology. Connecting + Sharing + Growing = Freedom.

You are the source of power, truth, and a balanced life. To find stability in this electronic age, we must define our equilibrium, social media symmetry, and interconnected parity. Our trail of sensitive data can be adjusted either intentionally, or unintentionally, while using the Internet.

It is inevitable that everyone at one point will be affected by cybersecurity issues in some fashion. The impurity disables our productivity. We need solutions to restore, reconstruct, and rebuild cybersecurity within our own lives. A "do it yourself" approach to breaking free from our Internet content. In other words, a natural treatment for our technology problem.

When someone repeats the same process continuously, the actions become instinctive habits. Therefore, we must regain control of our digital connection to understand the underlying problems. The solution lies within every person using a digital device.

We must become the practitioner of our problems and begin mending each facet of the inter-connected life. It is the equivalent to becoming your own virtual assistant. Only then can we create a happy and healthy existence with technology.

YOUR DIGITAL FOOTPRINT

The whole business internet model is broken; our free information-sharing highway has been hacked.

> *"Insanity is doing the same thing over and*
> *over and expecting different results."*
> ~ Albert Einstein

The original internet architects, engineers, and planners created a platform for people to share knowledge around the world. It's supposed to be an environment that could connect people from different cultures, races, business associates and such. But instead, digital information control is seeking to destroy this delicate multi-latitude database.

Unhackable is the true genuine cybersecurity solution that works on the interaction between the user and technology. It is the one controllable element that will put us back on course.

It does not matter if the technology is automatic or manually driven, you must know how the system is being manipulated to protect it from hackers. Therefore, the Unhackable mindset must be enacted. If the user does not understand the core processes of their system, then how can it be defended?

Users have a unique digital footprint that can be adjusted by using privacy and security settings correctly. Unhackable teaches users how to bring balance through intelligent actions while using Internet connections.

DIGITAL RESTORATION

Digital restoration is the beginning of the Unhackable program.

I will team up with the user or coordinator and incorporate
'The Elite Unhackable Program' for your data-driven digital life.

The program was designed with a fifty-two-day cycle to aid users in breaking the connective patterns of internet programming that will help build a stonewall of protection working in your defense. We can become the captain of our vessel. Do you want to be in control of your smart data?

THE TWELVE CHECKPOINTS

Internet connection is a manipulative and powerful force with the capacity to affect character development and behavior of its users. The effects can be seen whether users are in a public, private, or professional setting.

The world wide web plays an extensive part of our existence in society. Traditional business has been bypassed with the invention of the internet infrastructure. People from around the world can communicate to conduct professional services anywhere on the planet. It is without a doubt the greatest invention of our time. But it has turned humans into social media slaves who surf the super information highway void of any thought of the consequences.

The following section is the twelve checkpoints designed to restore the original programming while filtering malicious intent and unintended negative consequences forced on users through profit making-purposes.

Once the user establishes intuitive patterns, they can learn to maintain self-enforced discipline and keep them from the indulgences of Internet life.

1. **Helplessness** - The admission that technology has enslaved me, and I'm dependent on a data-driven lifestyle. Could I turn off your data-driven life for 48 hours?

2. **Connectivity** - The understanding that we are all connected; my actions impact others. The realization that my dependence on the internet affects me and everyone around me. Do I verify the validity of an email before its opened?

3. **Commitment** - The commitment to creating a quality of life that is in my control and not dependent on technology. Am I able to commute without technology and be mindful at all moments?

4. **Introspection** - The examination and observation of my processes to discover weaknesses and strengths related to technology. Am I aware of my environment while connected to protect my privacy and security settings online?

5. **Weakness** - The resolve to uncover internet deficiencies and weaknesses to learn about common failures. Do I stop to read license agreements?

6. **Desire** - The desire to avoid trigger points that generate the cravings and yearnings of my digital life. Can I stop clicking on those pop-up ads, and think before I act?

7. **Seeking** - The seeking of knowledge on how my digital life has been influenced in my daily routines. To neutralize and change these points to work for me and not against me. Can I control the technology or does the technology control me?

8. **Willingness** - The willingness to learn and grow while keeping my sensitive data secure. Am I ready to make the necessary changes and stay away from the questionable things online?

9. **Life** - The implementation of new modifications in my daily life that will directly affect my digital footprint in a positive manner. How can I modify my online behavior?

10. **Continuity** - The maintenance of ongoing focused patterns of behaviors that correct my actions in daily life. The desire to always be in full control and sustain power over my decisions to the connected world. Am I ready to stop the tracking of my sensitive data?

11. **Contemplation** - The commitment to anticipate how I consciously interact over the internet. To always be aware of my habits when dealing with new technology. Can I dedicate the time to make the necessary changes, and regularly change my passwords?

12. **Collaboration** - The responsibility to become agents of change to the things I have learned. Collaborate in a unified fashion, and take back control of our sensitive data, and online identities. Technology should allow us to connect, share, and grow, as it helps our life become less complicated. Am I ready to manage my own data and keep my personal information private?

In Summary:

Restore by educating yourself! The user must free themselves from all online intelligence, data gathering information, controls, filters, cookies, etc. The action will bring forth a paradigm shift designed to survive the test of time, and speed of innovation. It raises us beyond the failures of today's complex technology.

Reconstruct your private offline identity. Begin the initial steps towards rebuilding and renovating life online for all 'Internet of Things (IoT)', connected devices, etc. Create transformational mindfulness, throughout the internet, in a reinvented world full of incisive decisions. The user can learn to control technology, not have technology control the user.

Rebuild a life online by looking through a different lens. By establishing an interconnected shell, the user can build a conceptual demarcation line that creates a segregated stonewall defensive system. Collectively the masonry is mortared by the individual constructing the stonewall that will help stop threats to the user's sensitive data. It's time to bring forth true privacy and security in an insecure world. Are you ready for the Unhackable mindset?

By acquiring the skills to outmaneuver the processes of today, as well as future electronic database expansion, we can reclaim our digital freedom. Thereby, we can defeat communication technology with great ingenuity.

About George

George Mansour has a unique and simplified approach to Cybersecurity. As a trusted IT specialist for more than 20+ years, he helps clients overcome the debilitating effects of Cybersecurity issues. These distinctive methods have allowed him to emerge as an industry leader for individuals and businesses seeking to find a more secure system.

Mansour says, *"My mission is to help others fight against malicious and damaging attacks. Data breaches happen to everyone, they are not subject to certain individuals or companies. Hackers seek the easiest possible targets, and for the most part, it's people who think they don't have anything of value to steal."*

George understands the imminent threat facing anyone connected online. His goal is to empower end users with the tools to secure their digital assets using proper protocols. He seeks to enhance the validity of his client's lives, by teaching them the basics of online security. The systems, products, and services he uses are designed to prevent a breach before it happens—preventative methods are always preferred. It is imperative that users become proactive, because a cognitive distortion has taken over our senses. We need a compass to navigate the internet in real-time, and develop a license agreement with ourselves that isolates our unique sensitive data.

George received a Bachelor of Science in Business Administration (BSBA) degree with a major in Computer Information Systems (CIS) from Suffolk University, along with a Microsoft Certified Professional (MCP) certification. Besides his academic accomplishments, he is the founder and owner of CEHIT, INC., an acronym for Computer Engineering Hardware Information Technology – an Information Technology company that helped manage complex IT environments for over 15 years. CEHIT, INC. has been helping thousands of consumers and businesses (small, medium, and large), across the globe and continental USA. George Mansour focuses on numerous vertical markets and organizations in the healthcare, law, insurance, and manufacturing industries, etc. He has affiliations with partners and value-added reseller programs. Cybersecurity is a shared responsibility.

George's message is marketed with a global mission that technology interaction affects everyone. We are interwoven over the Internet as one, but individually unique. The Unhackable mindset creates the conceptual model to enact a multi-layer digital union between the technology and human interaction. The insecurities and impurities that threaten us online with every new connection must be controlled through a collaborative approach that will suppress the threats to our sensitive data. He says it's time to reclaim our digital lives and our digital freedom.

Mansour adds, "People are being hacked, have had their data stolen, been victims of identity theft, or had their computers held for ransom, all because they lack the proper understanding and importance of education, training, security procedures and having protocol processes in place that must always be dynamic."

As the risk due to espionage increases in an insecure world, so will the need increase for better security programs and systems that will also adapt with every new unknown that lurks at every twist and turn on the Internet.

You can connect with George at:

- Email: info@georgemansour.com
- Website: https://georgemansour.com

CHAPTER 9

HOW TO AVOID BEING HELD RANSOM AND PREVENT COMPLIANCE HEADACHES

BY MILAN BARIA

A recent report by the FBI shows that in 2018 alone, more than 351,000 cyber complaints were filed with reported losses in excess of \$2.7 billion dollars. The top three crimes reported for the year, were non-payment/non-delivery, personal data breach, and phishing schemes. Moreover, within the healthcare sector during 2018, over \$28.6 million dollars in HIPPA fines had been settled primarily as a result of data breaches.

Small business such as medical practices and financial brokerage firms can be subjected to pay large fines for non-compliance. The costs rise significantly if they experience a data breach or become a victim of a ransom-ware attack since lawyers, consultants, forensic experts and public relations support would likely be involved to help mitigate the exposure. Whether fined for non-compliance, or forced to pay a high ransom amount, the financial threats related to cybersecurity are real.

But the negative consequences are far more severe than just the financial blow. In fact, most organizations that have a data breach, never fully recover from the reputation damage and lack of trust that follows suit. For a pharmaceutical company, the theft or leak of intellectual property could be devastating for drugs still in their pipeline. Even if the organization manages to survive the first year after a breach, their clients, investors and the public often lose faith in the company's ability to safely secure confidential information and simply go elsewhere. The unfortunate impact of a cyber attack not only robs businesses economically, but instantly erodes the trust and reputation that may have taken years or even decades to build – with just a single data breach.

RANSOMWARE, ENCRYPTION AND CRYPTO'S

Today, cybercriminals are gaining control of computer networks, collecting information, selling data, and rendering files useless by encrypting them so nothing is accessible. The criminals will demand a ransom in exchange for releasing the company's own files back to them. It's not just happening with enterprise and hospitals these days, but small business all over the country. According to Cybersecurity Ventures, ransomware damages in 2018 will cost more than $8 billion dollars and predicts that 2019 damages will exceed $11.5 billion – with a ransomware attack made on businesses every 14 seconds.

As these kinds of news stories continue to break, more small business owners are becoming aware of the seriousness of these attacks. When a business does become compromised, the only way to unlock files that were encrypted is to pay the ransom with no guarantee your data will be returned. The sad reality is, some ransomware is so sophisticated that once a network is compromised, it's almost impossible to regain access to encrypted files—not even by a specialist provider, or the FBI for that matter.

To protect themselves the attackers generally demand payment via Bitcoin or some other form of crypto-currency, which makes it difficult for traditional law enforcement tracking to follow. Hackers originally targeted companies that clearly had money such as enterprise, hospitals and financial institutions. As the larger organizations adapted and invested in security and monitoring, the hackers moved to target small to medium-sized businesses that tend not to invest in those areas until it's too late.

Hackers commonly use automated tools to scan the Internet to see which businesses have vulnerabilities such as misconfigured or unpatched firewalls, servers and websites. When they find one that does, they breach the network to infect, track, steal or manipulate your information. They can do this from the comfort of their own home halfway around the globe. In today's everything internet-connected world, not making cybersecurity a priority is an enormous, avoidable mistake that can close a business in just a few minutes.

UNKNOWN AMOUNTS OF "DWELL TIME"

One of the tactics that these criminals use after penetrating a network is to watch activity before doing anything malicious, with you completely unaware. As such, employees continue to perform their normal tasks including accessing confidential information, ePHI, intellectual property, and other delicate information, providing the hacker a look at the businesses' most valuable and sensitive data.

Here is an interesting story: There is a business in my area that was hacked. The attacker had been watching their network activity for months building a profile on them under the radar. He eventually encrypted their files and demanded a large ransom. The company's CFO responded by saying they could not pay the ransom because they couldn't afford it. So the hacker, having been collecting data for months before the locking their files, then sent them a copy of their own financial statement from the previous month, and he said "You have plenty of money. You can afford to pay." Although the company had a backup system in place, it was also encrypted so they ended up paying the ransom.

The time from when a hacker gets into a network and actually does something is unknowable. It may be a day or two, or maybe several months or more. That unknown amount of time where a hacker has undetected access to a network to when they are completely removed, is called the "dwell time." During the dwell time, they could be doing anything from collecting information, reviewing files, or scanning account and social security numbers to analyzing how you and your office works, or leaking information to a competitor or regulatory agency. This may be all totally under the radar and undetected if your network isn't properly protected and proactively monitored from a security standpoint.

THE DANGERS OF SOCIAL ENGINEERING & PHISHING

The best network security and monitoring in place won't protect a business from what today is usually the weakest link – the human factor. Social engineering utilizes people's natural inclination to trust by manipulating them to give up confidential information. This is commonly done in conjunction with email phishing which together has a higher success rate.

Let's say a hacker wants to compromise a company or individual. Through basic searches on the Internet, they can find public information on someone via their own social media profiles, such as LinkedIn, Twitter and Facebook.

And if you are not savvy, a lot of times people will unknowingly put sensitive information online without even thinking about it. This is information that hackers can use against you to break into your own accounts or send phishing emails to you or your contacts with details that seem to "authenticate" the email, which gets users to open the emails and click on links or provide information.

A lot of the social media platforms have pop up quizzes and surveys that people take for fun and share with friends. These are questionnaires that are really common, and they ask users to answer fun questions such as, do they remember the street they lived on when they learned to ride a bike, or if they recall where they first saw their husband or wife. These usually appear harmless, so people answer these questions without even thinking.

Well, if you notice, these are the kind of security questions that are very common to the same kind of questions that a bank would be asking you to confirm your identity, or if you applied for a credit card. Such as, *"What is the name of the street you grew up on? Where did you meet your spouse?"* All those types of things are pieces of information that these hackers can piece together with other data to reset your online passwords or establish accounts under your identity such as a credit card.

So the hacking does not have to be through your actual computer. They can develop a composite profile of you, through social engineering and complete everything without touching your network.

FROM RADIOSHACK TOYS TO LUCENT EXECUTIVES

I started playing with IT as a kid. I was always interested in technology, and during the 1980s would play with electronic kits and gadgets from RadioShack. From there, I mastered custom car electronics installations. In fact, in the early 2000s when Lucent faced several challenges such as SEC violations and a stock plunge, several of their executives received death threats. I was actually involved in a covert operation installing one of the first vehicle control and GPS tracking systems that allowed the ignition to be cut remotely as well as door/window control and activation of onboard microphone and speakers – this later became what is known as OnStar today.

Then, in the early part of my career, I worked for an Internet service provider in Princeton, New Jersey, that provided services to many large accounts including Princeton University. The state police and the FBI would come into our office in order to gain access to information such as IP addresses when there was malicious or illegal activity occurring at the university or at one of our client sites, since everything flowed through our systems.

Working alongside law enforcement and government agencies has been a common theme throughout my career. Even outside of my work in cyber security for highly regulated industries, I have been recognized for service in first aid, as an emergency medical technician and volunteer firefighter, so I know the importance of cooperation necessary when partnering with local police and healthcare providers.

TAKE STEPS TO PROTECT YOUR SECURITY TODAY

Organizations with regulatory compliance requirements, such as those that are healthcare providers, broker-dealers, and bio-pharmaceutical companies, have the biggest risk if compromised and are prime targets for cybercriminals. Since the methods and steps these organizations must take to secure their networks are often state-of-the-art, non-regulated businesses can benefit by implementing the same standards to ensure they remain just as secure and protected.

Through my firm, Blueclone Networks, I help clients stay ahead of ever-changing technology and navigate the progressively complex IT compliance and security standards, by providing guidance and ensuring the appropriate tools, policies, and technology is in place.

With regards to action steps for this chapter, you can begin by deciding to take steps to protect your network security, today:

- Ensure all software and hardware firmware is updated continuously and monitor for new updates.

- Perform penetration testing and network auditing at least annually, and immediately after any significant change to infrastructure.

- Ensure your critical systems and files are backed up offsite via continuous, encrypted chain-free backups with appropriate retention periods.

- Ensure the appropriate IT Policies and Guidelines are in place for your industry and enforced. Update them annually and after any major infrastructure change.

- Establish a company program providing annual staff training on safe IT practices and a review of your company's IT Policies. Include frequent Security Awareness training such as a monthly tips newsletter and sending fake phishing emails to test employees.

- Ensure your business has the IT Security mechanisms in place with monitoring and remediation overseen by a vetted Security Operations Center, or "SOC".

- Most importantly – if your organization does not have the resources to complete the above properly, engage with an IT Services and Security Company that can work alongside your IT staff or act as your IT Team.

Having the proper Layered Security, Training and Backup overseen by the right team are key factors in not leaving yourself vulnerable to cyber-attacks and compliance violations. With proper planning, you can avoid data loss, hefty fines, reputation risk, unnecessary lawsuits, and financial insolvency, or even worse, an untimely business close. You can avoid being held for ransom.

We utilize an array of specialized technical, compliance and security experts gracefully packaged as a Comprehensive

Business Solution for our clients. Our plans are fully customized for each organization according to their structure and needs, designed to either co-manage or fully manage a client's network, security and IT compliance program. Some plans even include a $1 Million Ransom-ware guarantee and $1 Million in Cyber Breach insurance coverage.

From the initial client onboarding to ongoing high-level business reviews, we use a consistent, documented process built on ITIL and NIST framework to strengthen your program, complimented along with our wealth of experience. And best of all, you can rest assured that our process is adjusted continually to evolve, as new technology and regulations develop.

About Milan

Milan Baria is CEO of Blueclone Networks, has been certified by Microsoft and CompTIA, and is accredited in specialized areas including Cybersecurity and HIPAA. His wide-ranging experience in network security for regulated environments includes organizations governed by HITECH, HIPAA, FDA (21CFR Part 11), FINRA, and PCI-DSS.

He always had a passion for technology growing up and officially started his profession in the 1990's as an IT Consultant for a Technology Firm, quickly advancing to management within the Datacenter NOC of a multibillion-dollar Internet Service Provider, and then heading IT operations for a multinational pharmaceutical company. During his career, he worked with law enforcement agencies such as local police, state police, and the FBI on technology-related matters as well as with out-of-state cybersecurity firms seeking guidance or a local presence.

Outside of the technology sector, Milan is a husband and father that enjoys detaching from technology to refresh and relax by enjoying the outdoors through mountain biking, skiing, fishing and photography. Milan's adventurous side has included activities such as whitewater rafting, sport fishing in the Canyons, photographing an active volcano, canyoning, hang gliding and kart racing. He's explored over 20 countries including India, from where his parents immigrated.

Milan's travels abroad are primarily influenced by his longing desire to connect with others and learn about various cultures. He takes great pride in helping others in his local community and around the world through his company's philanthropic program. He is well respected in the local community, recognized for his past service as a volunteer Firefighter and NJ State Certified Emergency Medical Technician. While serving as Crew Chief, he was elected and served as President of his town's First Aid Squad where he worked with local government, police, healthcare providers and hospitals.

In 2006, Milan founded Blueclone Networks, an IT Services & Cybersecurity Company headquartered in Princeton, NJ. Milan's past work with law enforcement and within regulated environments steered the company's focus towards helping organizations within the healthcare, biopharmaceutical, and finance industries meet and demonstrate their compliance to regulatory agencies. His volunteer work in Emergency Services greatly influences the company's priority that ensures clients are prepared for emergencies with proper contingency plans, and can demonstrate business continuity and continued operation in the event of a natural, hardware, or security disaster.

To learn more about Milan, visit: www.milanbaria.com

All royalties from this book are being donated to St. Jude's Children's Research Hospital.

CHAPTER 10

AVOIDING HEADACHES, FINANCIAL LOSS, AND DIMINISHED TRUST WITH CLIENTS

FOLLOWING ARIZONA'S DATA BREACH NOTIFICATION LAW

BY DARREN PATONI

How to Avoid Headaches, Financial Loss, and Diminished Trust with Your Clients by Following Arizona's Data Breach Notification Law

Early in 2018, the Arizona Attorney General's office and Arizona legislators were looking at a compiled list of data breach notification laws from all fifty states. In terms of toughness, Arizona was towards the bottom of that list and because no one wants to be known as the state that doesn't enforce consumer data protection, the Arizona Attorney General's office decided that they wanted to update the law.

Arizona House of Representative T.J. Shope was the primary sponsor for AZ House Bill 2154. I had the opportunity to meet him along with the Arizona Chamber of Commerce, who opposed much of the early language in the bill, and helped to better define what implications it would have on businesses.

Arizona Governor Doug Ducey signed HB 2154 on April 11, 2018, amending and strengthening the states "Data Security Breach Notification Law." The new law, which took effect on **August 3, 2018**, can penalize businesses $10,000.00 per person affected by a breach with a maximum penalty of $500,000.00. In addition, businesses are required to notify clients and the Attorney General within 45 days after a security breach has occurred, making this data breach notification law one of the most comprehensive, pro-consumer, and toughest in the country. Many states are pushing similar legislation and the rest of this chapter will explain how laws like this affect businesses, and what you can start doing today to better protect yours.

In Arizona, any businesses entity, public or private, has a significant $500,000 liability for any data breach involving personally identifiable information. So if your business gets hacked and fifty client data records are stolen, at $10,000 a person you could be fined for the full amount. This is a significant liability and risk that could take many small and mid-sized businesses under if they don't protect themselves. What's worse is that you have forty-five days to notify the Attorney General and all your clients, of the fact that you had a breach.

Unfortunately, data breaches are on the rise. Not only will laws like these cause hefty fines, but if you are compromised, the reputational damage from trust lost with your clients could be insurmountable.

THE DOUBLE STANDARD FOR BIG BUSINESSES

Regrettably, there's somewhat of a double standard when it comes to data breaches and large corporations. Recently, Marriott's guest reservation system was hacked, exposing 500 million guests information.

The breach exposed names, phone numbers, email addresses, passport numbers, date of birth, and arrival/departure information. Millions had their credit card numbers and expiration dates compromised.

Sadly, small and midsize businesses often become complacent when they hear that another "corporate giant" was breached. They think if Marriot, Yahoo, eBay, or Equifax can get breached with all of their resources, then what chance does a small or mid-sized business have in protecting themselves? It should be noted that the majority of these breaches were entirely preventable.

A common factor of low visibility, along with inaction on the part of upper management, led to these compromises. Stolen and compromised credentials, from individuals with low-level access, allowed hackers direct access.

It seems that every week we hear about another huge cybersecurity breach, from where our confidential information was compromised. And yet, large corporations make some adjustments and continue right along. They have an established brand, deep resources, and incredible marketing engines. A $500,000 liability or fine is not a great impact on them.

Small and mid-sized businesses, on the other hand, can crack under that kind of financial pressure. Having to notify all your clients of a data breach is going to lose trust with them. This double standard definitely exists, and clients may never want to do business with you again if you don't protect their information.

Frankly, most business owners aren't aware of their states data breach law. Not being aware of the law is not going to help you if you get hacked and have a data breach. The Attorney General has the authority to prosecute business owners for a data breach.

ACTION STEPS YOU CAN TAKE TODAY:
LESSONS FROM INTERVIEWS WITH
OVER 60 SMALL BUSINESSES

Over the course of the last few months, I've interviewed over sixty companies and discovered a number of alarming realities. First of all, most people tend to use the same password (or some slight variation) for everything. This is extremely dangerous and very poor practice. Even if you slightly differentiate each password, this habit makes it rather simple for cybercriminals to pick you off like low-hanging fruit.

Many executives and business owners are overwhelmed at having to maintain all of these different passwords, so it's easier for them just to have one password for everything. This greatly increases the risk of being compromised. Because hackers usually take the path of least resistance, a dark web search for your company's domain name can reveal that your credentials have been compromised. This discovery uncovers that your Yahoo or LinkedIn account, was breached and now that login information is available to them.

By the way, if you are using the same password for your Marriot account, or any breached online service for that matter, that you are using for other online services (Office365, G-Mail, Internal Domain login, Word Press, Online Banking, etc....) you will want to change those immediately.

All too often a hacker searches the dark web to find that your consumer-grade file sharing utility account was breached. So, they now have this information and gain access to other applications like your customer database or your financial software package. Gaining access now requires very little effort because they have your login credentials. So, if you are using the same password for everything and one account gets breached, automated scans and scripting techniques rapidly expose other accounts you have that are now unprotected.

STEP 1: UTILIZE STRONG PASSWORDS

Throughout my interviews, I noticed that most people are unaware that security tools exist that can help you manage and utilize strong passwords across multiple sites and services. As a business there are a number of things you can do proactively to protect your information and deal with this liability. There is real risk involved here and there are really only three things you can do with this type of risk:

1. **Accept the risk** - In my opinion, this is like burying your head in the sand. However ill-advised, lots of business owners and executives choose this path every day.
2. **Transfer the risk** - In some cases, you can transfer a portion of this risk to a third-party or through cybersecurity insurance. There are still significant liabilities here if you have a breach and must notify customers or authorities.
3. **Mitigate the risk** - There are several things you can do immediately to diminish the risk associated with cybersecurity data breaches.

STEP 2: TRAIN YOUR EMPLOYEES

The first thing that you have to do is train your employees. Make sure that they understand the necessity of having strong passwords and know how to recognize an e-mail phishing attempt intended to gain access.

During my interviews, I heard several stories of businesses affected by fraudulent wire transfers. When a person's credentials are compromised and a cybercriminal gains access to their email, the criminal then sends an email impersonating the business owner or CEO of the company to an internal employee, requesting them to make a wire transfer.

In one case, $50,000 was transferred from an internal office person to a hacker using an email from their boss. The employee didn't have an alternate verification process or policy in place to confirm this was indeed a real request from the boss. All they had to do was pick up the phone and call their boss to confirm whether this was a legitimate transaction or not, and the hacker's plan would have been foiled. That's why one of the questions on most cybersecurity insurance applications asks if you have a secondary mechanism in place to verify the identity for any requested wire transfer of funds.

One of the biggest risks that any business has today isn't necessarily what firewall they have, or what end-point protection they are using. These are crucial cybersecurity tools, and you absolutely need them. Effective cybersecurity has multiple layers of protection including firewalls, backup, and security event and information monitoring. However, the greatest risk to any small or mid-sized business is their employees. Even good employees with good intentions will make big mistakes if they aren't given access to cybersecurity awareness training.

The right kind of training can help employees recognize a phishing attempt in which a hacker is trying to get them to click on an e-mail link designed to capture their user ID and password, or one that could install ransomware or malicious software on the network.

Let's say you have an employee who receives an e-mail that appears to be from Apple confirming their recent purchase of a $30 app. The email contains a PDF receipt attachment. The entire e-mail is a phishing attempt.

Clicking on the PDF reveals what looks like a receipt from Apple. At the bottom of the PDF, there's a "helpful" link with a note that says if you did not authorize this transaction, you could click the link to get a full refund. Clicking on the link brings the user to an exact replica of the Apple Account management portal.

If you enter your login credentials, you'll get a message that your account has been locked for security reasons. The hackers now have another set of credentials!

You have to train your people so they can know how to recognize these types of threats.

STEP 3: SEARCH YOUR COMPANY ON THE DARK WEB

It is absolutely imperative in today's business environment to use a service that will search the dark web on your company's behalf for compromised credentials.

The Dark Web is a sublayer of the Internet that is hidden and unindexed by typical and conventional search engines. Google, Bing, and Yahoo only search 4% of the indexed Internet. The other 96% of the Web consists of databases, private, academic and government networks, and the Dark Web. It is estimated that the Dark Web is 550 times larger than the surface Web and growing. Because you can operate anonymously, the Dark Web holds a wealth of stolen data, illegal activity, and is a cesspool of cybercrime. It is a place where online criminals can buy anything at auction within the cyber-underground.

Hackers can buy a person's identity, Social Security Number, credit card information, or email login. Also, this information is continually being updated and regurgitated back and forth and sold amongst hackers.

For the longest time, it was only the bad guys who had access to this information. However, the good guys can now access the dark web as well. Under a subscription model, the good guys can search the dark web for a business domain to see if the business has any compromises. Moreover, if they do have compromises, you can do something about it and immediately update those accounts.

During my interviews, I was able to share the results of dark web scans with business owners. In one instance I discovered that the business owner had his credentials breached. When I asked him if he was using this particular password for anything else, the owner said, "Darren, I'm using that password for everything." Needless to say, we spent some time discussing better "cyber-hygiene."

Compromised credentials that are bought and sold on the dark web reveal some very weak passwords. It's never a good idea to use family or pet names in your passwords. People can find that information out pretty quickly just by looking at your social media profiles. Social media surveys are another way that hackers can find out confidential information about you. So be cautious and conservative here. Some of these surveys are identical to secondary security questions for online password resets when you forget your password.

Once your compromised credentials are on the dark web, you don't get off the dark web. All that information is out there being publicly shared with criminals. What you can do is change and update your user ID or passwords and use this as another compromise detection mechanism.

STEP 4: UPGRADE TO NEXT-GENERATION ENDPOINT PROTECTION

Antivirus is essential, but antivirus only protects you against what it knows about. Antivirus is kind of like getting the flu shot. Some people get the flu shot every winter season, hoping it will protect them from that season's version of influenza. However, the shots can sometimes be 10 – 15% effective, and unfortunately, many people still get sick. Moreover, some people never get the flu shot, and they don't get sick at all.

Most antivirus software solutions only protect you against what they know about in their database of virus signatures. In today's cybercrime world, a hacker can take a known virus that an antivirus could detect, and they can modify it by changing one thing, and now it is a whole new and undefined, zero-day virus. Antivirus cannot adequately protect you if it doesn't recognize this new virus signature or scan everything.

So, I recommend that people replace their antivirus with next-generation endpoint protection, which uses artificial intelligence, machine learning, and deep learning, to understand what is going on in the computer systems to protect systems better.

STEP 5: MAINTAIN A DNS FILTERING SUBSCRIPTION

As another initial layer of protection, DNS filtering can circumvent many malicious websites designed to steal your information. DNS stands for the Domain Name System, and it is like the internet phone book, resolving every domain name with an IP address. Cybercriminals prey on human error and will craft replica logon websites that look identical to sites you use every day.

A DNS filtering subscription can help protect you from many types of online scams and malicious sites.

STEP 6: REGULARLY UPDATE YOUR SYSTEMS

Ensuring you have regular, systematic, security patches and updates on all of your computer systems today helps keep your systems running smoothly. Having proactive security updates and incremental patches applied regularly is crucial for any device on the Internet. All those devices have to be patched up and maintained to protect you.

These are just a few of the precautionary steps that business owners can take immediately to protect themselves. In addition to having a good backup and disaster recovery solution, you can mitigate this risk and avoid the hassle, headaches, and costs associated with not following new data breach laws.

About Darren

Darren Patoni is founder and CEO of The I.T. Workshop headquartered in Gilbert, Arizona. Serving the metropolitan Phoenix area since 1999, The I.T. Workshop is recognized by the Phoenix Business Journal Book of Lists as one of the Top Computer Consultant Companies in the surrounding Phoenix area and has been featured in *Entrepreneur®* Magazine as one of the "Top 100 Brilliant Companies To Watch" for Managed Information Technology.

Darren is an entrepreneur, sought-after speaker, and seasoned business leader. He is extremely passionate about helping small and mid-sized businesses protect themselves with effective Information Technology and cybersecurity solutions.

He grew up in a family of "fixers" and loves to help businesses contribute more value to their world by freeing up resources such as time, energy, and money through the use of innovative technology solutions. As a problem solver with numerous IT and cybersecurity certifications, Darren and his team of experts have created an innovative cybersecurity solution for businesses called Cyber Care.™

He graduated from Arizona State University, and early in his career became the IT Director for the Donor Network of Arizona, a federally-designated organ transplant and procurement organization. Darren has a keen understanding of "Mission Critical" technology and how to implement it in today's competitive marketplace.

Darren is an industry analyst for transformational technologies and a scrupulous research junkie. He has a unique ability to recognize tomorrow's technology today, and how that will affect small and midsized business in the future. He enjoys serving on local and national boards contributing thought leadership, policy guidance, and innovative growth solutions.

When not helping others protect themselves from cybercriminals, he can be found at the beach surfing, doing laps in the pool, SCUBA diving, skiing, or dirt biking.

You can connect with Darren at:

- Email: Darren@itworkshop.com
- Twitter: https://twitter.com/theitworkshop
- LinkedIn: https://www.linkedin.com/in/itworkshop
- Website: https://www.itworkshop.com
- Tel: 480.894.8640

CHAPTER 11

PROTECTING YOUR OFFICE 365 ENVIRONMENT

BY CATHY COLOFF

CYBERSECURITY TOOLS AND BEST PRACTICES TO HELP KEEP YOUR ORGANIZATION SAFE

As a business owner or manager, I know that you want to make sure that you keep your organization safe and keep your information secure.

I started my career at Exxon, and even back then, they were sticklers for security and control. You couldn't do anything without it going through change control – and this was back in the 1980s, long before cybersecurity was even a thing. So, I was well-grounded in security protocols very early on and they have been part of my IT-DNA ever since. Now, as Founder of IT Radix, security is one of our top priorities as a Managed Service Provider and outsourced IT department for the northern New Jersey area's small-to-medium-sized businesses.

At IT Radix, we always begin with the client and put their specific needs first. Then we will custom design solutions to fit their unique needs. Because most small-to-medium businesses (SMBs) don't have the same budgets that large corporations do, even though they have the same security needs, we adapt our recommendations and services to best fit the needs and challenges of our business clients. One platform we often recommend when discussing security requirements is Microsoft's Office 365 environment.

SECURITY STEPS FOR OFFICE 365

Microsoft Office 365 is a great platform for SMBs and organizations, because it gives them access to many of the same technology solutions that larger corporations have, but at a price point that's reasonable for their budget. Because there are so many features in Office 365, it can be daunting to know where to start. Most organizations typically start by using Office 365's email platform and extend from there. Let me outline a few key steps we recommend in Office 365 to enhance your security profile.

STEP 1: THE BASICS – SECURE YOUR EMAIL

(a). Have a good email filtering and advanced threat protection solution.

Our first focus is to secure your email flow. That means you want to make sure that you have email filtering. And not just your traditional junk email filtering, but also advanced threat protection which blocks malware threats and viruses. The various Office 365 subscriptions include different levels of advanced threat protection or, alternatively, you can also purchase it separately.

What does the threat protection solution actually do? Well, if you click on a link in an email that sends you to a webpage, it will check the link before it'll take you there. If it thinks it's something bad, it will post up a warning asking if you are sure you want to proceed. This warning is intended to make sure you really want to continue to a potentially threatening or harmful website. You can still continue if you choose, but if you do, then you are accepting the fact that you're going into an unsecured area.

Either way, we want you to have both filtering and advanced threat protection in place. Are you wondering why you would want to acquire these services separately even though you can get them through Microsoft Office 365? Because you will have the benefit of two different perspectives on what is considered a threat or malware. So, between the two solutions, you can broaden your scope of protection.

Of course, we want to protect you on all your devices and platforms. So, you need anti-virus or threat protection on each machine or device, in addition to within email. This is another reason you may wish to use a separate anti-threat solution, because it expands the scope of its protection beyond Office 365 to your entire device or machine. Think of it as a two-for-one deal. That means whether you have a PC or a Mac, an Android or iPhone, you always have some level of anti-threat software in place scanning at the operating system level as well as the email level.

(b). Turn on Outlook Safety Tips.

Another email security layer inside of Outlook is Microsoft's "Safety Tips." These tips use a traffic light analogy for flagging messages, but you must turn on "Safety Tips" because they are not set "on" automatically. The tips indicate if an email is something that can be trusted by flagging it green for safe. If the email is potentially spam, then the flag is yellow. If not, you have an option to identify a message as not spam. "Safety Tips" will also identify something that it thinks is a phishing scam.

Phishing is often an email scam, but it can also be found on websites. An example of email phishing is where you receive an email that may say something like, "Your email has been compromised. Click here to change your password." But when you click, it sends you to a hacker's site so they can capture your credentials and use it for their ulterior purposes. Often, they will try to trick you through social engineering into releasing information. Train yourself and your team to be on guard always. With the "Safety Tips" enabled, if Outlook thinks it's a phishing email, it will red flag it, warning you that this could potentially be a phishing email.

(c). Properly configure your DNS.

Next, we recommend setting up DNS (or Domain Name Service) to help secure your email. I like to think of DNS as "the telephone operator" of the Internet. When you want to send me an email message, you type my email address, your computer will ask DNS to look it up, and then tells your computer how to route the message through the Internet much like an operator directs phone calls. DNS has features to help prevent junk mail from being sent through and to help prevent something called "spoofing."

Many of us have experienced receiving an email message that looks like you sent it to yourself. Or maybe you got an email from a friend or family member, where it looks like they sent it to you, it has their email address at the top, but it's not a legitimate email message. That's spoofing. It's somebody that's pretending to be you or someone else. But if you set up your company's DNS properly, you can help minimize the ability of people to masquerade as someone else in email.

These three items are the basics, or the ante if you will, in securing your Office 365 environment.

STEP 2: KICK IT UP A NOTCH

Use Email Encryption.

Taking email security to the next level includes encrypting email messages. While you can do this for all email, sometimes it makes sense to do so only for individual messages. For example, basic email communications typically do not need to be encrypted.

There are a few ways within Office 365 to encrypt email. You can set up a policy at the server level that monitors every email, looking inside to see if it contains sensitive information, such as a credit card number or social security number. It scans the body of the email looking for potential patterns and words and, when identified, it encrypts the message automatically. The receiver will receive an email that doesn't just show their social security number right away, but rather they must request it to be unencrypted after a verification process. This encryption policy is at the server level.

But you can also allow that individual sender to decide when they have something sensitive to send in their message. In this case, they can type out a keyword. We usually encourage people to use the square brackets and put the word 'encrypt' in between, like this "[encrypt]"; so that when you do that, it triggers the email server to encrypt the message based on the user's judgment. This moves the responsibility for encryption from the server to the user.

Another type of encryption available is for key vendors, clients or partners that you communicate with regularly. If desired, you can set up "always on" encryption through the connection between your email server and your vendor or client's email server. For example, we have some clients that work with customers in the life sciences and biopharmaceutical industry. Quite often, we're asked to set up encryption between them for an "always on" encryption connection between the two companies. This is called "TLS" or Transport Layer Security.

All these types of encryption are included in the Office 365 platform and we encourage our clients to kick up their security posture by using encryption.

Turn on Multi-Factor Authentication.

Amp up your security even more by using multi-factor authentication. The idea is that you must have multiple pieces of information to validate who you are when you log in to the Office 365 environment.

This could be for when you can check your email in Outlook, or it could be when you're trying to get into your data stored in OneDrive or SharePoint which are part of Office 365. When you go to log in, you will be asked to type in the password, if it isn't already saved, then it is going to ask you for a second piece of information, usually a verification code to let you proceed through.

This verification code can be sent to your mobile device, an app on your desktop or even a special key fob. There are a number of ways to do it, but multi-factor authentication adds another important layer of security to your business system.

Why would you want to enable multi-factor authentication? Let me share a story about a local business that had a horrible experience before they enabled multi-factor authentication. Here's what happened. There were two people involved at the company – one was the account manager and the other was the financial manager. The account manager requested to buy some promotional material for an event that they were hosting, and the financial manager was acting as the purchasing agent. They made the initial request with the vendor, and there was some basic dialogue back and forth. But about halfway through the email thread, the vendor says, "Ok, wire us your transfer payment here."

Fast forward about a month-and-a-half, and the vendor came back and asked, "Why haven't you paid your bill?" And the company was surprised and replied, "What are you talking about, we paid our bill several weeks ago." When they started digging into it and looked a little closer, the financial person, somewhere about midstream through the email's transaction thread, noticed that the email address that they were communicating with had changed from the original vendor's email. The correct letters for the vendor were "dmc" – but they were changed to "drnc." In the lowercase, and being really close together, the "r" and "n" looked like an "m."

So, the company realized that they had been communicating with some other third party altogether, and they didn't even know who it was! It all started with the hacker accessing the account manager's email account months earlier and automatically forwarding the messages from the company to an unknown Gmail account. The hacker waited until the desired money transfer situation occurred. Ultimately, the company lost $40,000. The account manager's email account had been easily accessed because multi-factor authentication was not on.

STEP 3: AMP UP YOUR OFFICE 365 SYSTEM POLICIES

Turn on Auditing, Data Loss Protection and Rights Management.

The next step is to amp up your security even more at the top level. With Office 365, you can set up system-level policies similar to the server-level encryption rules. In the story above, if the company had disabled automatic forwarding rules this may not have happened. The other thing that helps is to turn on mailbox audit logging. This will allow us to find out who has logged into your mailboxes, sent messages and more.

Another tip is to use email archiving so that every message that goes in and out of your email server is captured in the email archive. And since most of these things are not turned on by default, it is a good idea to have an outside IT company come in and set them all up.

There are also file-sharing capabilities inside of Office 365 that offer document libraries and electronic file folders. There are two additional security features that you can enable – called Data Loss Protection and Rights Management. Here's how it works: If you had a client list stored in Office 365, you could use these features to safeguard that file. If I tried to email the file to my personal account or perhaps someone else outside of the company, the file could not be opened because I wouldn't have the permissions to get into the file unless authorized by the company's system policies.

Office 365 is a wonderful tool for businesses. But you need a professional IT consulting company to help you configure and enable the security features and ensure that you are doing your due diligence in protecting the information of your employees and customers alike.

About Cathy

Cathy Coloff is the founder and owner of IT Radix. Cathy and the IT Radix team have delighted New Jersey businesses with reliable, adaptable and impactful IT consulting and support for many years.

Cathy has diligently pursued her passion for helping organizations grow their business through the use of technology for over 30 years. Her driving passion is to increase clients' ability to grow revenue and profits through the implementation of reliable and cost-effective technology solutions that enhance productivity and security.

Cathy first 'cut her teeth' in technology at Exxon and Bear Stearns before entering the small-to-medium business world managing the day-to-day operations and technical service delivery for a regional IT company. From the beginning of her tenure at Exxon, Cathy was grounded in security and controls before cybersecurity was even "a thing." She recalls weekly meetings to review upcoming changes in the Exxon computing infrastructure and their impact on security and operations. At that time, the security concerns were primarily focused internally because the Internet was not even in use. As with many things in life, timing is everything and for Cathy, rolling out the first local area network in the Exxon ECS company led to many opportunities in the future to gain knowledge, experience and expertise in the various operational and security concerns facing organizations today.

Cathy founded IT Radix in 2008 and is a hands-on business owner. As IT Radix has grown, she has worked in almost every position at IT Radix including as its first technical consultant. While she no longer carries a "toolbox," she has over 30 years' experience selecting, implementing and supporting business technology. She can talk the talk because she walked the walk.

From the early viruses to today's sophisticated social engineering attacks, IT Radix has assisted its clients in identifying and pro-actively addressing its operations and security as a Managed Service Provider (MSP) and more importantly, as technical consultants. In 2018, IT Radix was named to the CRN MSP 500 list as a leading Managed Service Provider in the Pioneer 250 category. In 2017, IT Radix was recognized as one of the IT service industry leaders in New Jersey's Morris County being named as one of the "Best of the Best."

Cathy graduated from Duke University with a B.S. in Electrical Engineering and went on to obtain an M.S. in the Management of Technology from Stevens Institute of Technology. Cathy was recognized as one of NJBIZ's **2018 Best 50 Women in Business** and as one of the **Top 25 Leading Women Entrepreneurs in New Jersey**. Additionally, she is a member of numerous trade organizations and technology mastermind groups. She often mentors young engineers, as well as other business owners and managers, in the information technology industry and beyond.

When not helping organizations grow, Cathy enjoys sailing, cross-country skiing and relaxing in New Jersey and Vermont with her husband, Doug, and son, Alex.

You can connect with Cathy at: cathycoloff@it-radix.com or check out the IT Radix website at: www.it-radix.com

CHAPTER 12

YOUR MEDICAL PRACTICE: DEFENSE IN LAYERS

4 WAYS TO STRENGTHEN YOUR PRACTICE'S IT SECURITY TODAY

BY TERRENCE BOYLAN

...there are only two types of companies:
Those that have been hacked and those that will be.
~ Robert Mueller[1]

Think of your medical practice as a small business, because it is indeed just that. Research conducted by the National Cyber Security Alliance found that:

1. Almost 50 percent of small businesses have experienced a cyber-attack.
2. More than 70 percent of attacks target small businesses.
3. As much as 60 percent of hacked small and medium-sized businesses go out of business after six months.[2]

---

1. https://www.brainyquote.com/quotes/robert_mueller_826981
2. https://www.inc.com/thomas-koulopoulos/the-biggest-risk-to-your-business-cant-be-eliminated-heres-how-you-can-survive-i.html

123

While the particulars of each case certainly vary, the reasons for these businesses' insolvency due to technology-breached circumstances are largely the same. There is often a financial burden due to HIPAA-related fines from the Office for Civil Rights (OCR) ranging from $100 to $1.5 million.[3] The cost of remediating such a breach is currently $408 per patient record.[4] The overall loss of reputation in the community and resulting stunted future practice growth is really the final straw. A practice can't buy that back.

Many times, the fines, malpractice suits, and recovery costs resulting from data breaches alone can exceed a practice's insurance umbrella. Moreover, the breach may be so severe that it takes out all the practice's IT systems so that they do not have the ability to recover in a timely manner. The resulting trouble, financial burdens, and regulatory implications from cybercrime can overwhelm your practice, your staff, and ultimately, you.

THE COSTS OF A RANSOMWARE ATTACK

Unfortunately, physicians frequently assume that basic mechanisms like HIPAA compliance or a firewall are enough to protect their medical IT systems and online Electronic Medical Record (EMR). However, the sad reality is that it's simply not true. To help improve your medical network and online systems from cyber-attack, this chapter will provide some practical tips to help you strengthen the safety of your Protected Health Information (PHI).

For starters, one area to consider improving is training for your staff. Often, the greatest security threat your practice faces stems from your own staff. Especially, in the IT space, it is widely known that employees who do not follow proper protocol can be the weakest security link in your practice.

3. https://www.beckershospitalreview.com/healthcare-information-technology
/10-common-hipaa-violations-and-preventative-measures-to-keep-your-practice
-in-compliance.html
4. https://www.healthcareitnews.com/news/ransomware-malware-attack-breaches
-45000-patient-records

Why are a physician's staff their largest security vulnerability? It is because they are subject to well-targeted ransomware attacks, which only escalate should the targeted practice pay any money to the attacker. Eighty-one percent of cybersecurity incidents are caused by employee negligence. Perhaps an employee uses weak administrative sign-in credentials or even shares credentials with other staff. Maybe a laptop which wasn't fully encrypted was stolen or lost. Or maybe the employee clicked on a phony email, attachment, link or download, exposing the computer and network to malicious software. No matter the reason, it spells big problems for healthcare providers.[5]

Some best practices to review include:
1. Requiring unique and strong passwords for each employee
2. Regularly changing passwords
3. Verifying security on new and existing computers
4. Continuously training tenured as well as new employees

Because the digital landscape is constantly changing, there are countless variables that, if not addressed, may leave your practice vulnerable. So, you need always to be checking for new vulnerabilities – probably not the reason you started your medical career.

FOUR DEGREES OF SEVERITY

There are four levels of pain, or degrees of severity and consequences, that can occur by not having secure IT systems and procedures in your practice.

1) Operational Inefficiencies

The first degree is the pain of not effectively conducting business and operational inefficiencies. This would include events like staff downtime or a network outage. Or maybe

---

5. https://cyberpolicy.com/cybersecurity-education/4-healthcare-cybersecurity
-stats-thatll-raise-your-blood-pressure

your computers are not online, and you cannot view a patient's bloodwork or CT scan. Or maybe your staff cannot process co-payments, file insurance claims, send electronic prescriptions, access your secured email, schedule patients for follow up visits or check patients in for their appointments. These are the basic services your practice and staff require to function daily. Because you handle such personal and sensitive issues for your patients, they expect your systems to have no downtime and little delay.

2) Organizational Fines

The second degree of severity would be the fines that are put on a healthcare provider, from the OCR or even the Federal Bureau of Investigation (FBI). The financial burden due to HIPAA-related fines ranges from $100 to $1.5 million.[6] The situation can get dire and costly very quickly without proper protection and documentation.

3) Patient Fallout

The third degree of severity which can be extremely damaging is patient fallout. A lack of confidence from patients leaving you, to patients sharing what happened with the community either by word of mouth or through an online review results in lost reputation and strained relationships in general. I call this a "reverse referral" or an "anti-referral." It is a negative review of your practice and costs you patients, rather than gaining them.

4) Resulting Lawsuits

Finally, in extreme cases, patients may outright sue you. Generally, a privacy breach suit comes in the form of a malpractice suit. It is at the top of the list of worst-case scenarios and most provider's greatest fears. Once one

---

6. https://www.beckershospitalreview.com/healthcare-information-technology
/10-common-hipaa-violations-and-preventative-measures-to-keep-your-practice
-in-compliance.html

patient sues for malpractice, it can cascade into a flood of lawsuits from other patients whose data has also been compromised.

Remember, nobody hacks a system just to access one patient's record. Cybercriminals want to take _all_ your records, to extort money from you through a ransomware attack or sell them on the dark web.

> "...Information like birthdates, Social Security numbers, and driver's license information are used to fill out, submit and validate any number of fraudulent accounts or transactions – such as income tax filing, financial aid applications or insurance claims. Marital status or emergency contact and employment information can also be used to guess security validation or password reset questions. And email addresses or phone numbers can be used to evade anti-fraud mechanisms such as PIN systems or multifactor authentication."[7]

Also, just to put this into perspective, while the value of a social security number is only about ten cents and a credit card number is about twenty-five cents, the value of a health record on the dark web can be as much as several hundred or even thousands of dollars![8]

A well-positioned attack can wreak havoc, so you must be ready to defend your practice at all times. You must encrypt and test your backups, review your procedural documentation, and constantly run cybersecurity automation on all systems each day.

Cybercriminals must only be right once for them to gain access to patient data. However, YOU must be vigilant ALL THE TIME to stop them.

---

7. https://www.csoonline.com/article/3189869/data-breach/healthcare-records
-for-sale-on-dark-web.html
8. https://www.forbes.com/sites/mariyayao/2017/04/14/your-electronic-medical
-records-can-be-worth-1000-to-hackers/#2ec5f66550cf

PROVIDE DEFENSE IN LAYERS

A great way to protect your organization, patient's information, and yourself, is by understanding the need to defend your company in layers. Simply having a firewall is not adequate. Installing endpoint protection on your laptops and desktops is just the start. Encrypting all hard drives, backups, and web-based services is not enough. In today's climate of healthcare security breaches, you need defense in layers.

As the CEO of a multimillion-dollar, boutique IT firm that focuses on application, infrastructure monitoring and troubleshooting within the healthcare industry, I have seen it all. I have been hired by several large and very prominent healthcare organizations to design their wireless networks and wireless security. I have also been hired to assist the U.S. Navy in Iraq to train technicians on how to operate wireless networks safely and securely. We have a customer base that ranges from every branch of the military to civilian agencies, private hospitals, pharmaceutical companies, and biotech companies. These are organizations that have a very strong need for a stellar security posture. While you may not have the budget these multi-billion-dollar organizations have at their disposal, you do have the same needs. Here are four actions you can take today to improve your practice's cybersecurity stance.

1. Test Your Backups – It's the restoration that matters!

We primarily serve medical professionals in Rhode Island, focusing on helping their practice effectively use technology while keeping their data secure, staff well-educated, and patients happy. It is not enough only to have a backup. The backup must be encrypted. The backup must be continually tested and retested for its ability to fully restore your critical systems in a timely manner. Ask yourself, "Does my backup get me up and running quickly enough? Is the time to fully recover a server or workstation as fast as I need it to be? How long am I willing to be out of business?" If it takes you a day or more to rebuild your servers should an attack take place, then, in my opinion, it is not an adequate backup. Services needed to run your practice should be fully operational in minutes, not hours or days. All these processes can be and should be fully automated, including the testing.

2. Continually Audit Your Devices

Whenever we take on a new client, we always have an initial fact-finding discussion. Many times, clients will realize they are facing weaknesses which may not have been taken into consideration before. Now, we are there to advise you on steps you can take to protect your network and your patients. Again, that all comes out of the initial discovery meeting. After that, the next thing we do is a scan of your network and devices. This audit will look for vulnerabilities which may exist, and configuration vulnerabilities which are present. Then, the next step is to create a remediation plan. We will come up with a plan together to fix and repair any gaps in your security system. We will also rerun the audit to gain confirmation that our remediation has indeed fixed what we said we were going to fix, and that everything is working correctly and securely. This entire workflow can be done remotely 24/7 by a competent healthcare-centric IT provider.

3. Ongoing Data Monitoring

Another essential step to include in a security system is daily data leak monitoring to limit access to PHI. For instance, if somebody has attacked your system, has begun accessing your files, and has also covered up their footprints, then you may not know it until a patient finds a text file with all their patient information on some out-of-date server. In 2007, this very incident occurred at Westerly Hospital.[9] The largest source of threats may come from your own staff. For example, an employee may illegally access a patient's

---

9. https://pbn.com/westerly-hospital-data-breach-affects-200023678/

record because they know that person.[10] Routinely check your computer and server logs for all log-in attempts and views of patient data. There are various services available that do just that. Lastly, you can monitor for PHI on the dark web. While continually looking for any of your patient's data on the dark web may not be why you went to medical school, it is an effective safeguard for your practice. Any reputable healthcare-focused IT provider should be able to offer you this service. Just remember: a patient's health record is immutable: they can't just cancel it like they can with a credit card. Once it is out there, it is forever a risk.

4. Regular Staff and Provider IT Security Training

Finally, a key component of your plan which often goes overlooked is IT security training. Every one of your employees, staff, and providers should undergo, at the minimum, annual cybersecurity training. Options range from in-person sessions at your offices to online videos and testing. Every person worthy of your training dollars should be tested. There are tests which each person takes online with immediate scoring and suggested study. Several services are available which test your staff through fake phishing emails to see who opens a questionable attachment or clicks on a suspect link. The results are then shared with you and your IT provider to develop a plan for correction. Constant training is critical to the success of your IT plan.

HELPING PEOPLE NOT HURT THEMSELVES IN IT SECURITY

My passion is to help successfully merge the medical profession with technology, keeping your staff, providers, patients and you safe – enabling your practice to have a long, productive, and profitable life.

---

10. https://www.beckershospitalreview.com/healthcare-information-technology
/10-common-hipaa-violations-and-preventative-measures-to-keep-your-practice
-in-compliance.html

Some of the horror stories in IT security sound extreme. And not all of them necessarily have a malicious undertone. Sometimes events occur where a computer vulnerability was left open to attack by a simple mistake or an oversight. Sometimes it is just plain ignorance that has resulted in tragedy. Other times, a clinician inappropriately accesses a patient record for a benefit of some sort.

Today's medical climate is very complex. From insurance filings, government reporting, patient care, practice management, digital EMR like Epic™ or eClinicalWorks™, to continuing education, there is a lot for you to think about and juggle. Far more than doctors from a previous generation.

There is qualified IT security help available to medical practices. This is not a losing proposition. You can adequately protect yourself, your staff, and your patients diligently on a daily basis. You can win this game. Working with a seasoned, local, healthcare-focused Managed Services Provider is a great place to start.

About Terence

Terrence Boylan is a passionate Information Technology Executive, Entrepreneur, Speaker, Author, and IT Strategist. He is the Chief Executive Officer of PacketLogix, Inc. of Warren, Rhode Island, which he founded in 2003. Terrence is a cum laude graduate of Harvard. In 2018, he became an Alumni of the Goldman Sachs 10,000 Small Business Program.

From the age of ten, when he rewired his parent's antique house so that he could have a telephone in his room, Terrence has understood the practical application of technology to solve real-world problems.

As a stockbroker for Lehman Brothers, he led his peers by automating sales and marketing programs with a very large and clunky laptop computer – bleeding edge technology for the late 1980s.

As Director of Marketing for non-profit estate planning associations in Boston, he was responsible for the complete overhaul of all IT systems, development, deployment and administration of the largest database of insurance providers in New England. He worked diligently to keep all systems up, running, and available for business. It was in this position, he learned about and understood the real value of "system availability" – a term which would later define his future enterprise, PacketLogix.

In 2003, Mr. Boylan formed PacketLogix, Inc. with the sole aim of providing tools and solutions to enterprise customers throughout the northeast. In the close to two decades of practice, PacketLogix has attracted an impressive list of discerning customers from large pharmaceuticals and Ivy League schools to hedge funds, as well as all branches of the United States military, and even The White House in Washington DC.

Mr. Boylan has been hired to travel to Baghdad, Iraq to help design, troubleshoot, and train US military contractors on networking and wireless networks for the Morale, Welfare, and Recreation program under SPAWAR for the US Navy. He has worked in other middle-eastern areas remediating various networking problems.

Terrence Boylan is very active with local Boy Scouts. During his spare time, he can be found fishing, hiking, or camping with friends and family. He lives in the East Bay of Rhode Island with his wife Jennifer, and two amazing and energetic boys.

You can connect with Terrence at:
- Terrence@PacketMedical.com
- www.linkedin.com/in/terrenceboylan/
- www.packetmedical.com
- Tel: 401-329-8762

CHAPTER 13

DO NO HARM

BY ALISON MEREDITH

BLOWING THE WHISTLE

In 2016, the Office of Civil Rights received a hot tip which said, in effect:

> "You should inspect this particular medical office. Two years ago, they had a HIPAA breach: two laptops were stolen. Instead of reporting everything the way they should have, they covered it up. I know they were covering it up because I work there, and I watched it happen. This has been nagging my conscience ever since, and I am finally letting you know. What they did is not right."

I'll bet you can guess what happened next. OCR showed up on the office's doorstep to ask about the incident and begin a full investigation of the company's HIPAA compliance. The medical office admitted to the security breach, but also explained that they had followed all appropriate steps, both to mitigate the damage and to notify appropriate authorities.

Who was right? What really happened?

The whistleblower was a disgruntled former employee. Her

complaint to OCR was her vengeance on the company which had fired her. However, OCR did not care that this whistleblower had an axe to grind. The complaint she filed was all the evidence their team needed to open a full investigation.

HARMFUL NEGLIGENCE

The official term used by the OCR is "willful negligence." Disregarding HIPAA compliance or, more importantly, the security required to obtain that compliance, is negligence. Serious, harmful negligence. Do you think "harmful" is too strong a word?

Consider how you would feel if:

> ➤ A random person read all the details of your medical history
> ➤ An estranged member of your family read all the details of your medical history
> ➤ Your identity was stolen

What if one of those things happened *and* you figured out that the origin of the crisis was a medical office doing a sloppy job protecting your personal information? Would you consider yourself "harmed" by that medical office? What would you think? What would you do?

MORE VALUABLE THAN GOLD

In September 2011, someone broke into the locked car of an Adult & Pediatric Dermatology employee and stole a thumb drive containing protected patient information. That stolen thumb drive, which probably weighed about 1 ounce, turned out to be over *a hundred times more valuable* than an ounce of solid gold.

Hard to believe? An ounce of gold is worth more than $1,200. But Adult & Pediatric Dermatology agreed to a settlement of $150,000, for privacy and security violations related to deficiencies in its HIPAA compliance program.

Mike Semel, author of *How to Avoid HIPAA Headaches*, summarizes this concept well:

> "You can't ignore or keep delaying risk management. Organizations have paid millions in fines while trying to save thousands in remediation . . .
> . . . If you think of DATA as GOLD, and stop thinking of data as bits and bytes, you will do a better job protecting your organization.

> - Gold has a high value. So do medical records.
> - Gold needs to be secured. So do medical records.
> - Gold is something criminals want to steal. Like medical records.
> - Gold is worth over $1,200 per ounce. Medical records are worth much more."

HIPAA Compliance, in a nutshell, is about having this mindset toward your patients' data. Your patients expect a standard of care from you: wash your hands, don't reuse needles, etc. They also expect you to guard their Protected Health Information.

HIPAA COMPLIANCE IS COMPLICATED

The market is flooded with Do-It-Yourself solutions. "Just fill out this checklist" is the main sales pitch for most of them. They assume a Security Risk Analysis is simply a list of things to read and check off.

Suppose you are managing an office of pediatricians, and a new partner has an idea: a checklist, mailed to new parents just before each baby's 6-month birthday. He explains, "Parents would make the observations listed, check them off, and then mail the completed page to us. We could look over it before billing the insurance company. The babies would still have the benefit of getting their well-child checkups completed, but think how much time we'd save!"

Ridiculous! Of course you'd never ask new parents to complete comprehensive DIY evaluations of their babies. Evaluating the development of babies is so complicated that people spend years in medical school and residency learning how to do it.

Evaluating whether your organization conforms to both the Privacy Rule and the Security Rule of the Health Information Portability and Accountability Act is also complicated. You cannot do it yourself.

A GOOD HIPAA COMPLIANCE CHECKLIST

To comply with HIPAA, you must:

1. Complete a thorough Security Risk Analysis, both annually and after significant changes to your network or office environment.
2. Create an Action Plan for addressing any weaknesses revealed by the SRA.
3. Follow the Action Plan you created.
4. Train your team regarding HIPAA Compliance, annually.

The details of the first three steps are complicated, as I have just explained. However, the good news is: you don't have to do them on your own. Your HIPAA Compliance recipe can be simple, if you stir in one key ingredient.

THE CRITICAL INGREDIENT IN YOUR HIPAA COMPLIANCE PLAN

The key to keeping your HIPAA Compliance simple is choosing the right vendor to help you.

You must choose a third-party vendor who:

> ### Knows the intricacies of the law.
To properly interpret and follow this law, you need someone who understands the Health Insurance Portability and Accountability Act and all its ramifications. A vendor with expertise in IT or Practice Management, but whose HIPAA education is sparse, will not suffice. Instead, your vendor must employ people who have read HIPAA and who stay abreast of recent judicial rulings.

> ### Knows the intricacies of cybersecurity.
Other chapters in this book expound on this. Ever-changing threats require your security defenses to be frequently updated and maintained.

> ### Provides a convenient, easy-to-use system to pursue compliance.
Their solution should not get in the way of you managing your practice. Instead, it must provide a user-friendly way for you to record and reference policies, procedures, Business Associate Agreements, the status of each employee's training, and progress on each action item from your Security Risk Analysis.

NOT IF, BUT WHEN

Not too many years ago, cybersecurity providers talked about what happens if you get hacked, if there is a data breach, or if someone alerts OCR that you may not be compliant.

We have recently changed our tune. We now use the word "when," especially regarding HIPAA compliance:

- When you have a breach, even if only of one patient record (mistyping that fax number).
- When your EHR software company informs you that a

breach has put your patients' records at risk.
- When the OCR gets a tip that they should investigate you.

You need to be prepared to respond to a breach and/or an investigation, not because it might happen, but because it almost certainly will.

CAUSES OF DATA BREACHES FOR MEDICAL OFFICES

1. **Hackers.** Although this is the most famous cause, everything else on this list is actually more likely to happen to you.

2. **Careless employees.** Here in Northeast Tennessee, a Wellmont nurse disposed notes on over 1,700 patients in a public recycling bin. Was she trying to be earth friendly when her office had a "clean up" day?

3. **Malicious employees.** Have you heard the one about the nurse who was fired? Her boss let her go without first blocking her access to their network. So, before waving her last good-bye, she accessed their Electronic Health Records (via connecting to their Wi-Fi, from her car parked next to their office) and downloaded some information she could sell on the dark web.

4. **A Vendor.** The data center of your cloud-based EHR vendor could be hit with ransomware, or someone cleaning your office could grab paper notes accidentally left on the desk of a busy doctor.

RANDOM ENFORCEMENT IS NOT WHAT YOU SHOULD FEAR

I have often heard doctors or practice managers say, in effect, "We're just a little fish in a big sea. OCR doesn't have time to audit everyone. I'll just take my chances that they won't ever audit me."

There is a grain of truth in this perspective. The resources devoted to enforcement are relatively small when set against the long list of businesses which must comply with HIPAA. However, this mindset shows a lack of awareness about the risks of non-compliance.

Whether or not OCR knocks on your door does not depend on whether they randomly pull your business name from a hat with thousands of other options. Instead, it depends on whether someone alerts them that they should pay you a visit.

You must prepare for one of these actors to contact OCR, requesting that you be investigated for noncompliance:

> Concerned patients
> Current employees who are disgruntled
> Former employees who want to punish you
> Unethical competitors
> Vendors

When the OCR gets a tip from anyone on that list, they will pay you a visit. Don't expect them to notice or care how valid the complaint is.

THE REST OF THE STORY

Let's get back to that story about the terminated employee who contacted OCR to exact revenge. The person who filed the complaint fades into history, after getting (almost) exactly what she wanted: her previous employer was punished. The punishment? Thankfully, only this: enduring hours of headaches responding to the query. Art Gross, president and CEO of Secure Now, summarizes the event:

Thankfully, the medical office targeted by that disgruntled employee *actually had* completed a Security Risk Analysis annually *and* had clear documentation to show it. When the two laptops were stolen, they followed proper security procedures, documenting what was done and filing necessary reports. Although hours of time were lost as we helped them respond to OCR's questioning, their investigation ended positively. That's why I can tell you, "It's a true story, but the name of the office is confidential." The happy ending here is not simply that they did not have fines to pay, it's that they had *no reputational damage.*

If, on the other hand, OCR had found something wrong (if their most recent SRA was not recent enough, for example), even if that discovered point of non-compliance was unrelated to the stolen laptops which prompted the investigation, the company would have received both a fine and lots of bad press—prompting patients to take their business elsewhere.

THE IMPORTANT THINGS IN LIFE HAVEN'T CHANGED THAT MUCH

Computers are new on the scene of human history. The tools and methods doctors use every day are radically different from those used 50 years ago.

Yet the mindset of any conscientious healthcare professional is still the same: "First, do no harm." That famous phrase (generally attributed to Hippocrates) well summarizes how a provider should approach a patient's physical and psychological well-being.

It *also* summarizes how you must view your patients' data:

Don't intentionally put that data in harm's way.

About Alison

Alison Meredith is the co-owner of Holston Information Technology Company in Bristol, Tennessee. Holston IT specializes in providing cybersecurity and compliance solutions for medical offices and other businesses with strict regulatory requirements.

Alison earned a BS from Virginia Tech and taught Math at high schools in North Carolina, Tennessee, and Massachusetts. While teaching at North Andover High School, she was one of only ten teachers to receive the annual Future Leaders Award from the National Council of Teachers of Mathematics.

Alison paused her professional work to be a stay-at-home mom. She says of those years, "The skills I gained are too numerous to list, and the pay was priceless."

Alison and her husband Tim (a Microsoft Certified Systems Engineer) founded Holston IT in 2008. Holston IT is one of the top IT Services companies in East Tennessee and Southwest Virginia. They were recently recognized on the cover of Business Solutions magazine for their fast growth, excellent client service, and expertise in serving businesses which must comply with HIPAA.

Connect with Alison at:
- alison@holstonit.com
- https://www.linkedin.com/in/alisonmeredith7/

CHAPTER 14

SOCIAL ENGINEERING: WHY THE REAL THREAT ISN'T TECHNOLOGY

BY JASON MARILLA

I believe that IT and cybersecurity should be accessible to everyone. All individuals and businesses have become a potential target for cyber-crime. This is why I do what I do.

Teaching people how to be cybersecure is a passion of mine. When it comes to security, ignorance is not bliss. It is a liability. Unfortunately, most people and organizations believe that the technology from a few years ago is still enough to protect them today. This is simply not the case. Technology is always changing, so the need to continuously adapt and be 'security aware' is crucial.

Additionally, the malicious actors online are better equipped, better funded and more organized than ever before. Between state-sponsored attacks, organized crime and financially-motivated black hats, most organizations do not stand a chance without the proper cybersecurity solutions or the help of a qualified IT security professional.

However, nothing will change until more business owners make the decisions to be properly informed about their real options. My team and I seek to ensure that the veil over IT security is a little clearer for owners and managers to peek through, and make better decisions based on what they have learned.

THE LIFE OF A THREAT HUNTER

I am a managing partner for Axiom IT Consulting Canada. I am an enterprise architect with over 20 years of experience in the IT field and work as a cybersecurity team lead specializing in endpoint security and threat-hunting.

In order to hunt successfully, I look for system vulnerabilities and indicators of compromise on a network to find out if there has truly been a security breach, and how widespread it is in the IT environment. I describe threat hunting in layman's terms as "hacker hunting." I use special tools and threat intelligence to perform my hunts along with the help of retired military security analysts and like-minded technology partners to find and mitigate threats when needed.

I also work with the Joseon Group as a Solutions Consultant, where I use my skills and knowledge to advise clients on how to secure their networks using a continuous life cycle model while identifying how to secure the most vulnerable parts of their organization, along with the "human factor."

Threat hunting requires me to hypothesize on where threats can come from and where threats may exist in a network. The human factor will always be vulnerable from attacks through multiple means such as phishing emails or through direct physical attacks. A physical breach is when a hacker tries to gain access to a victim's computer to install malicious files or payloads. Therefore, my job is to consider how a company's employees could have unintentionally exposed their company to a system breach.

I have worked with small to medium-sized business, and major corporations in all aspects of IT, not just IT security. Some of my projects have been in the creation of e-commerce applications that generate millions of dollars annually for a client. In this case, any downtime they might experience could affect their stock price. Therefore, a securely-designed system was paramount as we worked in teams to achieve a common goal. As part of this team, the developer and I succeeded in creating the required environment to allow the application to function correctly in high traffic scenarios, allowing up to 50,000+ visits to the site per day.

I have been involved in several threat-hunting engagements that have allowed companies to discover unknown security breaches and hackers dwelling in their networks. The hunts helped remediate previously unknown issues and ultimately improved the company's security posture. I have worked with several top-tier cybersecurity firms to assist clients with everything from security risk assessments to ISO 27001 audit preparation.

Finally, I continue to work with Toronto Police Service on Information Security Toronto as a board member, a grassroots executive seminar series that seeks to educate C-level executives, business owners, directors and managers of organizations in the Toronto area about cybersecurity risks and solutions.

There is no such thing as 100% secure. Constant and continuous education is essential. Security is a delicate balancing act between function and protection. Too much of just one takes a toll on an organization. Therefore, balance is what I seek to uncover, while also emphasizing that security is not an event but an ongoing process.

THE HUMAN FACTOR: GREATEST STRENGTH AND GREATEST VULNERABILITY

Because of my background and experience, I have a unique perspective on how companies are leaving themselves at risk.

When I work with a business, I analyze their risk level and check for potential attack vectors. I ask them to tell me about their business. After interviewing them, I explain how I or a hacker would potentially break into their network and advise them on the next steps on how to protect their network.

I also explain that if I were to try and infiltrate their network, I would not come at the system with a straight technological attack. Breaching any network is always easier through the weakest link—the "human factor." I would gather information about the employees and the company, as well as anything and everything I could get my hands on, including what kind of systems are running, in order to determine ways I can use this information to penetrate the network.

For example, if I found that my target liked dogs, I would use this info to create a pretext and engage in establishing rapport. My objective would be to get you to comply with my requests – like clicking a link on a convincingly fabricated website about dogs that will install a malware to infiltrate the network once it was clicked on through a phishing email, or the intent could be for me to get the victim to enter personal data that allows me access at a later time. These simple attacks are considered social engineering, and it is a cyber-attack that leverages several tools to exploit human nature and emotion. Social engineering is the art and science of leveraging people in order to gain influence over them to perform an action that would provide an attacker access to their system.

From the earlier example, if the business owner was local, I would try to meet them in person and get as close as I could to establish rapport to look for ways to leverage the personal information I discover. Information such as their likes and dislikes can be used as leverage to do something that allows me to complete my mission of accessing their network. If I'm successful, he or she may not even be aware of the actions I influenced them to do.

HACKERS PREY ON THE EMOTIONS
OF THEIR VICTIMS

People are the weakest link in any security system because they can be tricked and their emotions manipulated. A highly effective social engineering attack is very specific and customized to the target. In my example, once you click the link that I am trying to bait you with, I actually don't care if I don't get your personal information right away. Once I'm in the network, my objective is to stay for as long as I can to try and gain further access. I would also attempt to social engineer others further by causing computers to function poorly. This poor performance usually prompts an administrator to log on to check, and I would then harvest their admin credentials to "live off the land" and have full reign over your business to establish multiple beachheads from which to obtain a stronger foothold on the network.

When I describe this process to prospects, it becomes clear for many of them that they don't have policies, procedures or solutions in place to protect themselves from this kind of a social engineering attack. I then remind them that there are solutions but there's also no such thing as 100% secure. I further tell clients that the best defense is to put up enough layers of security to potentially deter the efforts of an attacker or catch them in the act. With regular employee security awareness training, this can help them stay one step ahead of the hackers by building a security-conscious culture.

FOUR WAYS HACKERS CAN STRIKE

There are many ways to attack a network but social engineered phishing emails are the most common because they're effective. There are four common ways for hackers to attack businesses and individuals to install malware or install backdoors.

- The first technique is phishing, these are fraudulent emails usually meant to gain sensitive information through crafted messages that contain hyperlinks or attachments that, when clicked, allow a hacker to harvest passwords or gain access to your computer.

- The second way is through vishing, which are malicious calls to get you to do something. It's similar to telemarketing but meant to elicit information or scare you into performing actions for the attacker to take advantage. For instance, Canada was bombarded by many fake calls that claimed to be from the Canada Revenue Agency (CRA), which is the equivalent to the IRS in the U.S.A. The callers would try to intimidate recipients into installing software or giving them their credit card information. Unsuspecting victims that believed the threat of jail time or a large fine for a tax filing error could be addressed with their cooperation. Some of these scam calls were successful and some reports on these incidents went as far as to convince victims to not only send money but also gift cards for payment. Effective social engineering attacks prey on victims so well that odd requests like this worked. Canadian and Indian law enforcement teams continue to work on tracking down and imprisoning the perpetrators.

- Thirdly, there's smishing, which is basically a fake text message from a hacker posing to be your phone company or your bank in order for them to gain access to your private information online. Smishing is much like phishing, but it uses SMS messages as a way to deliver the messages.

- The fourth way is with a physical social engineering attack. A common example is when an auditor or attacker poses as a job applicant at a firm. Their objective is to either infiltrate the office facility to gain access or to deploy some sort of software physically to infect a computer with a remote access tool for them to use later on. In some cases, the auditor or attacker would approach the front desk receptionist to tell them that they are there to meet with Human Resources for an interview, but needed help to print their resume as they had spilled coffee all over it.

If the attacker/auditor has done their homework on the company, they would leverage their findings to get themselves in a position to either influence the receptionist to insert a USB key with their resume that holds a malicious payload, or find a way to gain access to the facility to drop off the USB key where someone could find it and potentially insert it in to their computer for the auditor or attacker to gain access remotely after they leave. This example is a common weakness for companies, but it is something that can be easily prevented.

SOME STEPS TO PREVENT SOCIAL ENGINEERING

It is important to note that social engineering happens all around us. From a child attempting to manipulate parents to do something for them to an effective marketing ad that leverages your emotions to buy products, the difference is that malicious social engineering attacks, like the CRA scam, tend to require some background info on their targets. The scam was likely the result of these criminals gaining access to previously-breached data. For example, information from department store breaches is found to be sold or exchanged on the dark web.

Malicious social engineers use all of the tools available to them to create a better pretext or back story when engaging their targets. A good pretext is what makes a social engineering attack effective. Therefore, it is important to arm your employees with the right skills and tools to defend your front line. Listed below are a few suggestions:

(a). The first thing that business must implement is a set of security policies. For example, policies or rules that ensure the receptionist doesn't let anyone into the office without verification is a good start. Companies have policies for their operations, and security policies are just as important.

Start with an acceptable use policy or develop a security policy on how to handle suspected phishing emails. The key is to set guidelines so that people aren't left to make a judgement call on their own. Start with the question of "Do my employees know what they need to do?" to get an idea of what your security policies need to be. If you are unsure, a security professional can definitely help.

(b). The second item that needs to be considered when creating policies is to ask, "Do my employees have the skills to follow the policies?" Simple issues that a security professional can quickly identify may not necessarily be obvious to your employees, and therefore it is essential to know what they need to be trained on and why.

Furthermore, once you have an understanding of your employees' skills and have implemented the policies, you must conduct security awareness training to reinforce your policies. In my opinion, blindly providing security awareness training is an incomplete solution. Some security awareness training services provide regular phishing email testing and online training videos for the employees, and this helps to keep security top of mind. However, in order to make your security policies more effective you have to make sure that the training provided applies to your policies and your employees.

Our approach is to provide instructor-led training reinforced with a good security awareness training program on a regular basis. This way, employees are trained on how to look for clues of social engineering, and to also have a better understanding of why the policies are implemented in the first place.

(c). Furthermore, there are technologies like firewalls, spam filtering, and advanced endpoint protection systems that can help protect your company even if social engineering attacks are successful. This book mentions several of those technologies. My advice is that you speak to a security professional to understand the technology options that best fit your company's operations.

(d). Last but not least, a professional social engineering audit would be a great way to determine how resilient the company would be to a social engineering attack. When a company understands the social engineering risks and how to improve its cybersecurity – these are significant steps towards creating a security-aware business culture.

Defending your small business from cybercrime is an ongoing process. By implementing these best practices, and training your employees on the threats around them, you will be in a much better position to defend yourself and your organization.

About Jason

Progress, not perfection! This is something that Jason Marilla, an established entrepreneur, enterprise architect, threat hunter, and speaker, has believed throughout his life.

In life, like technology, there is no such thing as perfect. "Realistically, driving for perfection is unreachable. Therefore, progress is a better objective in life and technology because it helps to avoid complacency." This was a catalyst for him to take risks, learn more and succeed faster right from the beginning of his career more than 22 years ago.

Jason started his career in IT in his teens and was fortunate to have worked with established IT professionals that mentored him in technology, security, and business operations. This exposure of hands-on training and education led to his understanding of enterprise networks and security that would serve him well later in his career.

His passion for security originally began as a hobby and became an obsession. This led to unconventionally-gained knowledge, while his education in Information Technology Management as a graduate of Ryerson University and Centennial College helped to enhance his skills to design and build IT systems for his clients with security in mind, while implementing business requirements.

Over the years, Jason's experience with large multinational institutions in diverse industries and his work with smaller IT Service Companies created a more experienced system architect. His natural talent to see patterns helped him to understand technology and programming languages, and also helped him recognize patterns in human behavior.

Jason's upbringing has always driven him to have a "provide-value-first" mentality, and as such, he works with the Toronto Police Service as an advisory board member in running a grassroots project called Information Security Toronto – which provides seminars and workshops in helping to educate business leaders on how to be more cyber-aware and secure.

He has lent his expertise as a speaker on subjects like threat hunting, endpoint detection and response, and security awareness for events hosted by organizations such as Microsoft Canada and the Toronto Police. Jason hopes to further educate business leaders on what companies can do to improve their security posture via his speaking engagements, grassroots projects and his involvement as a consultant with security firms like Joseon Group.

More recently, Jason is proud to contribute to this book. His input into the dangers of social engineering and the ways to protect organizations from the weakest link in any security system – "the human factor" – is something that companies must consider and pay more attention to daily.

In Jason's words:

"We hear of breaches daily and most attacks from hackers stem from the manipulation of human beings. Without proper security awareness and training, organizations will always be at risk. It's time to change."

You can connect with Jason at:

- J.marilla@axiomcan.com or www.axiomcan.com
- jmarilla@joseongroup.com or www.joseongroup.com
- jmarilla@infosecto.com or www.infosecto.com

CHAPTER 15

HELPING MANUFACTURERS GROW THEIR BUSINESS WITH BETTER I.T.

BY CLINT BRINKLEY

For manufacturing companies, or any kind of company for that matter, the reason that they implement a cybersecurity program, just like any security program, be it online or physical, is because they have a need to protect their people, their information, and that of their clients. In addition to excellence in security, manufacturers also need to protect their database and network, while maintaining optimal productivity.

We understand the need to balance these priorities. We don't want people to be exposed to undue risk, and we definitely don't want a client to lose valuable production time. The bottom line is that we must prevent cyber threats, quickly remedy tech-related issues, and do both as efficiently as possible for our clients.

We want our manufacturing clients to be able to keep working and not have to worry about their IT problems and online security. We don't want to have a situation come up where for instance, a CAD drawing of a very important and expensive piece of equipment is held ransom because proper security wasn't put in place, or that there wasn't training and policies for all team members. So there always has to be training involved with employees and procedures that minimize the risk of cybercrime.

As a result of putting the proper cybersecurity measures that we recommend in place, our clients remain safe. One of the companies that we work with builds very large equipment, and they had implemented an entire cybersecurity plan that we developed for them. But while they had already had Anti-Virus in place, it wasn't really protecting anything. And we actually found, by implementing our enterprise-level Anti-Virus and security software, that there was something laying up under the surface of about 75% of their computers in the company. And they were like a 200-person company.

Not only that, but we created a map of how all this was being communicated with the hackers. What we discovered was that it all tracked back to the accounting software. When we told the accounting vendor that they had a hole in their software, and it had created a vulnerability that was being hacked, they adamantly denied it until we sent them the information. After that, they said: "OK, we'll get back to you after our programmers fix it." So yes, there can be harmful situations going on in your business right now that you may not even be aware of. There are threats that can fly totally under the radar. And because this company went with a commercial grade security system, they thought that was going to be enough to cover them. Unfortunately, it wasn't. After we made some major repairs and updates, with minimal downtime, they were able to get back to business as usual.

BEST PRACTICES FOR TRAINING TEAM MEMBERS

I first learned about the importance of checking for viruses when I was in college. Back then when you would walk into the computer lab, everybody had to check their floppy disks at the door. As I went into my career, the first big instance of a virus hack was with a construction company that we serviced nearly twenty years ago. At the time, we didn't really know what to do or how to mitigate it. But what we learned over time is that there are ways that we can become more proactive with defending and preventing against attacks.

For example, now we have better Anti-Virus software and can implement appropriate policies and procedures to help educate end-users on the importance of preventing viruses. That's really one of the most important things to do, educate the end-user, because I have clients that literally email me on a daily basis saying that they received a notification of unusual activity on their account. And of course, they had a Microsoft account, and they had received a fake Microsoft notification as a phishing scam attempt.

So, it is important to have a policy that trains their employees on using common sense and best practices online. You should emphasize with your team that nobody should click on anything unless they are absolutely, 100% sure that it's safe. With that being said, we have clients who call us, email us, and forward stuff to us all the time, and of course, we will help them determine whether or not it is safe.

There are also email security features that we put into place for a lot of our clients. For instance, we partner with Barracuda Networks, and they are one of the top email security companies in the world. So we will put policies into place in that system that will require our clients to make sure that they abide with the email restrictions. So the email inbox is another layer, in addition to Anti-Virus that we help with. I highly recommend locking email down to a balanced point of maximizing protection with high usability.

On a stricter level, some companies have decided that email users need to have anybody that sends them an email message, to register

159

their email account on the company's server. So that means that if somebody that has never sent you an email before decides to message you, they will have to first sign up for an account and have you approve them before their email is delivered. That way you don't get any kind of outside solicitations or unverified promotions from people outside of your network. Even if a user who has emailed you before becomes compromised, and they send you a message, the system will check it and if they discover an embedded virus contained in the email, they will say no to the sender. So even if this person has messaged you before, the server will show that there is now cause for concern and they will block that message, and we will quarantine it so that it does not infect the server.

HOLLYWOOD HACKERS: MORE FACT THAN FICTION

We're also doing a lot right now to help our clients through spear-phishing. Phishing is basically just social manipulation. It's when a hacker or other cybercriminal will try to get you to initiate an action that is going to enable the hacker to compromise your system. This could be through a piece of monitoring software, or it could be a link that gets clicked in an email that enables the infections of a virus. These types of things can happen in a lot of different ways. And I've seen these things happen in real time. It's scary. People will click on a link without knowing any better and not realize it, but they've actually just compromised their whole system.

Hackers may have secretly turned on your computer microphone or your computer camera, and now they are recording everything that you say and do in the office without your knowledge. So if you're on the phone and you give somebody your bank account number or piece of other sensitive information, the hackers could potentially gather that info without you knowing.

It sounds far-fetched and sometimes a little bit like Hollywood, but these things are real, and cyber-cases like these happen every day. I know because my team and I are often called to remedy these situations on a regular basis.

Another attack that hackers will try is through programs that are called keyloggers. What keyloggers basically do is what their name sounds like, which is to log every keystroke a user makes. And if a keylogger gets installed on your system it can monitor every single keystroke that you make, so it will know every website visited, every account number entered, and it will keep track of every piece of information you type online. And these keylogger programs are notorious for reporting information back to the Dark Web. Once your information gets out in the Dark Web, it can't be taken back. Passwords and account numbers can be changed, but with Social Security Card and debit card information, the damage done can be irreparable.

That's why I recommend that people make sure that they check their system and scan it for viruses on a regular basis. It's also important to always be changing your passwords and to be updating your login information. Unfortunately, there are all these consumer products that are being sold, and just because people know their name from advertising, people will buy that product. But just because a product is well known doesn't mean that it works well. Actually, what that means is that it has become a very big target for all hackers.

So, if your software is a big target, that means that hackers are going after your product and they are trying to find holes in your system. And while that product may catch some of the old attacks, there are constantly new ways that hackers are developing to penetrate your system. So it is going to be much harder to catch these new threats because they will literally bypass the old Anti-Virus. There are just thousands of scenarios that can happen out there and so you really do need to protect yourself.

TIPS FOR UPDATES, NETWORK SCANS, AND PASSWORDS

Don't underestimate the importance of doing regular Windows updates. I try to convey to people just how important this is on a regular basis. Windows updates are necessary. I know they can be a pain in the neck sometimes, but knowing which ones to install and which ones to ignore is key. People have a tendency to either ignore all of them, or install all of them, and neither of those options is ideal, because not every update may be appropriate for your individual computer.

Another thing would be telling people to update their passwords on a regular basis. This is just something that everybody needs to do. However, even before you start resetting your passwords, you need to make sure that your systems have been scanned and cleaned recently. This goes back to not just having an Anti-Virus in place, but really having a higher-level security-type program that can look for rootkit viruses and other things that are not operating within the operating system.

For example, if you're using Windows and you reboot, a rootkit virus can re-infect Windows when you restart. So you need to make sure that your system is clean and has strong Anti-Virus. This will ensure that you don't have any keyloggers, malware, viruses or ransomware on your system. And as long as you can make sure that there are no keyloggers on there, I strongly recommend that people go through and change their passwords every thirty days. And don't just use "password" or proper names and birthdays, like those of your kids and spouse, because that information is usually pretty easy to find on the web via social media.

Another tip on passwords is to vary the length of your passwords. Keep them all various sizes, so that it keeps hackers guessing. This creates a level of complexity and makes it more difficult to break into your network. Also, consider using a combination of uppercase letters, lowercase letters, numbers, and symbols. Other tips for passwords would be to substitute letters for numbers and symbols. So for example, you can substitute the letter "O" with the number "0" or the letter "L" with the number "1".

VISION FOR A STANDARDIZED IT FUTURE

We have clients coast-to-coast. Right now, we're in about twenty different states, and we serve clients from all across the manufacturing sector. From asphalt companies to companies that supply parts for phone towers, from brickwork companies to machine companies, we serve them all.

And I'm happy to do so. Cybersecurity is going to be the major topic in business over the next five to ten years. One of the things that my company did was to discover a zero-day virus with one of our clients, and the hackers had attempted to take them down on Black Friday. This was one of our retail clients, so this attack would have been devastating to their business. However, we were able to notify them in time, and we are able to block all of that malicious activity. In the end, we were able to keep our client safe and running their business as usual. It was a huge success, and they were very thankful for our support.

We are also investing a lot into my staff right now, to actually train them to become certified, ethical hackers. These are the people that are called "white hats." They are the good guys. So you have the "black hats" which are the bad guys that you hear about in the news, and then you have the white hats, which are the people you want to have on your team. Because we are looking for the holes and inconsistencies in your network so that we can help plug those holes and prevent the black hats from taking advantage of you.

I started this company as a technician, but I'm not a technician by nature. I'm really more of a businessperson. I look at things from a businessperson's point of view, rather than a technician's point of view. I don't ever let any of my sales team or engineers go out to pitch a product or service. Instead, when we go in to see a prospective client, we start by discussing their pain points with them. We'll figure out how we can best help their company be a more efficient business. We'll go in looking for what ails them and address those shortcomings, rather than just try to sell something. So we come in as a consultant and help them grow their business, and we may be able to pinpoint ways that they can save some money, or train their people, and we just start with adding value before we get to the technology.

I really want to leave my mark on this industry. My vision is to see things become more standardized in the future. I want to raise the bar on what's accepted and required as an IT professional. I think there are too many technicians running businesses and technicians don't make good business decisions. Because of that, you see a lot of companies that may have a couple team members, but they are never really able to scale because they don't know how to get over that hump. They don't know how to be efficient, and they don't know how to grow their business.

I really want to make a positive impact on this industry. That way people don't just roll their eyes and speak poorly about their IT person, or treat them like second-class citizens. Rather, I want to train IT people to be seen as an asset. I want IT people to be seen as professional problem solvers who can fix things, and add value to their clients and the companies they work for.

About Clint

A self-described problem-solver on a tireless chase for success, Clint Brinkley is widely-known as a self-made man who understands that nothing good in business – or life, for that matter – comes without sharp determination and a thirst to excel.

As the CEO of Your Business Solutions, an industry-leading Managed Service Provider (MSP) and Cyber Security firm he co-founded in 2004, Clint knows that, for some, success comes in the form of forging the path for your own venture, learning from the mistakes of your predecessors, and building a business all your own.

The inspiration to build and create Your Business Solutions grew from years of working inside the IT and technology industry, and was, ultimately, born as the result of the tangling frustration of watching managers, CEOs, and business owners make poor decisions that dramatically affected their companies.

It was after (yet another) stint at a tech business that was brought to its knees by poor management decisions that Clint decided something impactful. If he was going to work for anyone and take ownership of both mistakes and successes, he was going to work for himself.

Through collaboration, observation, and taking several notes on "what not to do," Clint developed Your Business Solutions in 2004. Now, Your Business Solutions is expanding from their headquarters in The Woodlands, Texas into multiple cities and proudly serves dozens of clients across the continental United States.

The biggest influence for Clint – and the one to whom he credits his tenacity, determination, and drive – is his father, Ray Brinkley. From a young age, Clint took note of the continuous dedication his father allotted to several business ventures. It was from his father that Clint learned the building blocks of success: focus, self-sufficiency, and an emphasis on communication.

Beyond that, Clint credits the power of observational learning, self-education, and investing time and efforts into both his current success and future endeavors. While recognizing the importance of formal education for some, Clint credits his drive to self-motivating factors and continues to spend his time consulting with mentors, reading everything he can get his hands on (both his home library and Audible queue are overflowing), and seeking out relevant information.

But Clint's sheer, unrelenting drive for success isn't the only secret to his business savvy. Much of his business philosophy centers around taking ownership of everything – successes, failures, and everything in-between.

Clint's success was hardly overnight – in fact, it was over 20 years in the making – but with business, that's sometimes just the way it goes. For Clint, his success only came through creative problem solving, an over-emphasis on communication, and the willingness to anticipate and eliminate the obstacles in your way.

It doesn't matter how thick the wall is—Clint is always determined to go through it.